⫸ THE WEISS EDITION ⫷

Haggadah Shel Pesach
For Youth

With Explanatory English Translation
and Selected Insights from the
Rebbe's Haggadah

This Haggadah was created in loving memory of

ר' ישכר דוב ומרים וייס ע"ה
R' Yissochor Dov (Berel) and Miriam Weiss ע"ה

ר' שלום וצפורה לפידות ע"ה
R' Sholom and Tzipporah Lapidus ע"ה

Sponsored by

Rabbi Moishe & Ruty Weiss

Sherman Oaks, CA

MACHON MIYAD
על שם ישכר דוב ומרים וייס ע"ה

HAGGADAH SHEL PESACH FOR YOUTH

With Explanatory English Translation and Selected Insights from the Rebbe's Haggadah

A project of Tzivos Hashem, Jewish Children International: 792 Eastern Parkway, Brooklyn NY 11213

Sponsored by Machon Miyad in loving memory of R' Yissochor Dov and Miriam Weiss ע"ה

Published by Merkos L'Inyonei Chinuch: 770 Eastern Parkway, Brooklyn NY 11213

Orders:
291 Kingston Avenue / Brooklyn, New York 11213
(718) 778-0226 / Fax (718) 778-4148
www.kehot.com

The Kehot logo is a trademark of Merkos L'Inyonei Chinuch.
ISBN: 978-0-8266-0632-7
Printed in China

"כִּי־לִי בְנֵי־יִשְׂרָאֵל עֲבָדִים עֲבָדַי הֵם אֲשֶׁר־הוֹצֵאתִי אוֹתָם מֵאֶרֶץ מִצְרָיִם אֲנִי ה' אֱלֹקֵיכֶם"

(ויקרא כה, נה)

Foreword

This Haggadah is a very exciting addition to the Machon Miyad series. It includes a unique translation and explanation of the words of the Haggadah; along with the loose translation in bold type, the basic meaning of the text is explained in regular type.

It also contains insights, history, and stories selected from the Rebbe's commentary on the Haggadah. The explanations presented here are especially dear to us as Chassidim, because they are from those personally selected and written by the Rebbe. Although there are many explanations from all our Rebbeim, as well as many more explanations that the Rebbe said and wrote over many years, the commentary in this Haggadah is taken exclusively from what is known to Chassidim as "*The Rebbe's Haggadah.*"

Acknowledgements

We would like to thank the following people for making the Weiss Haggadah possible:

Rabbi Moshe and Ruti Weiss for sponsoring and spearheading the project; Rabbi Hersh Lasry for compiling the translation and explanation; Rabbi Shmuel Loebenstein for compiling and writing the tidbits, Rabbi Dovid Leib Chaikin and Rabbi Yosef Minkowitz for reviewing and editing the Haggadah; Fred Casden and S. Herz for editing the English text; Rabbi Shmuel Rabin for proofreading the Hebrew text; M. Wreng and N. Vukadinova for the illustrations; Rabbi Sholom Heidingsfeld, Rabbi Mendy Shanowitz and Rabbi Shmuel Vaisfiche for reviewing the illustrations; the team at Spotlight Design including Zalman Friedman, Moshe Muchnik, Zalman Stock, and C.M. Raskin for the layout and design.

Special thanks go to the directorship of Tzivos Hashem: Rabbi Yerachmiel Benjaminson, Rabbi Sholom Ber Baumgarten and Rabbi Gershon Eichorn, as well as the Editor in Chief of this Haggadah, Rabbi Zalman Glick, and the Director of Chayolei Tzivos Hashem, Rabbi Shimmy Weinbaum.

We would also like to give a special thanks to the directorship of Kehot Publication Society and their editorial staff for their help and insight in making this Haggadah.

We hope that you will enjoy using this Haggadah, and learn a lot from it. May we be zocheh to bring the Korban Pesach in the Beis Hamikdash this year!

Tzivos Hashem

Features of this Haggadah

EXPLANATORY TRANSLATION: Along with the loose translation in bold type, the basic meaning of the text is explained in regular type, so you can know both the translation of the words as well as what they mean in context. There are many ways to explain the text of the Haggadah. The explanations presented here are based on the Rebbe's commentary on the Haggadah.

The English explanation is not an exact translation of the Hebrew words. Therefore, it may not be used instead of the Hebrew words for any brachos, as you would not fulfill the obligations of these brachos if you were to say these words instead of the original Hebrew text.

HEBREW TEXT: Much of the Haggadah discusses pessukim in reference to galus and geulas Mitzrayim. The Haggadah will often bring a passuk, and then discuss the meaning of certain words or phrases in it. To help follow the meaning, the passuk is in bold, purple type, and where parts of a passuk are repeated and explained, they appear in regular purple type and have quotation marks.

For example, the Haggadah brings a passuk:

אֲרַמִּי אֹבֵד אָבִי, וַיֵּרֶד מִצְרַיְמָה וַיָּגָר שָׁם בִּמְתֵי מְעָט, וַיְהִי שָׁם לְגוֹי גָּדוֹל עָצוּם וָרָב.

After quoting the passuk, the Haggadah explains six parts of the passuk, beginning with:

"וַיֵּרֶד מִצְרַיְמָה," אָנוּס עַל פִּי הַדִּבּוּר.

TIDBITS: The tidbits included in this Haggadah are taken from the Rebbe's commentary, and are presented in eight categories:

A DEEPER LOOK

Reasons or advanced explanations.

DID YOU KNOW?

Interesting tidbits.

HISTORY

Historical facts or things we do to commemorate them.

MINHAGIM

Discussions on minhagim.

NUSACH

The significance of certain words or phrases.

SEDER OF THE SEDER

Explanations of the order in which we do or say certain things.

STORY

Stories of our Rebbeim.

WORD POWER

The meaning of a certain word or words.

Contents

הַגָּדָה שֶׁל פֶּסַח

סֵדֶר בְּדִיקַת חָמֵץ
SEARCHING FOR CHAMETZ

הַמִּנְהָג לְהַנִּיחַ פְּתִיתֵי חָמֵץ קָשֶׁה וְזַמֵן מָה קֹדֶם הַבְּדִיקָה כְּדֵי שֶׁיִּמָּצְאוּ הַבּוֹדֵק וְעַל פִּי הַקַּבָּלָה יֵשׁ לְהַנִּיחַ עֲשָׂרָה פְּתִיתִין. וְקֹדֶם שֶׁיַּתְחִיל לִבְדּוֹק יְבָרֵךְ:

וְצָרִיךְ לְחַפֵּשׂ לְאוֹר הַנֵּר בְּכָל הַמַּחֲבוֹאוֹת גַּם בִּסְדָקִים שֶׁבַּקַּרְקַע, וְלֹא יְדַבֵּר בֵּין הַבְּרָכָה לִתְחִלַּת הַבְּדִיקָה אֲפִלּוּ מֵעִנְיְנֵי הַבְּדִיקָה וְנָכוֹן שֶׁלֹּא יָשִׂיחַ שֶׁלֹּא מֵעִנְיְנֵי הַבְּדִיקָה כָּל זְמַן בְּדִיקָתוֹ וְיַעֲמִיד מִבְּנֵי בֵיתוֹ אֶצְלוֹ לִשְׁמוֹעַ הַבְּרָכָה שֶׁיִּבְדְּקוּ אִישׁ בִּמְקוֹמוֹ וְלֹא יָשִׂיחוּ בֵּינְתַיִם וְיִזָּהֲרוּ לִבְדּוֹק בַּחֶדֶר תְּחִלָּה לַמָּקוֹם שֶׁשָּׁמְעוּ הַבְּרָכָה וְלֹא יֵלְכוּ לִבְדּוֹק תֵּכֶף אַחַר הַבְּרָכָה לְחֶדֶר אַחֵר:

- The minhag is to put ten well-wrapped pieces of hard chametz around the home some time before the search that will then be found during the search and burnt the next morning.

- The search should begin after nightfall and be performed by candlelight. One should search even in obscure places, such as in cracks in the floor.

- The minhag is to use a wooden spoon, a feather, a beeswax candle, and a paper bag, all of which is later burned with the chametz.

- One should not speak between the brachah and the beginning of the search, even concerning the search itself. Throughout the search one should not speak about anything that is not relevant to the search.

- It is best if all adult males in the home participate in the search. They should stand near the head of the household to hear and say amen to the brachah. Each of them then searches one section of the home. They should all begin the search in the room nearest the place where the brachah is said and only then go on to search other parts of the house.

HISTORY

שַׁבָּת הַגָּדוֹל

Shabbos Hagadol—the Great Shabbos—is called so because of the great miracle that happened on the Shabbos before B'nei Yisrael left Mitzrayim.

The Egyptians found out that Hashem was going to kill all the firstborn-sons, and to avoid this, the firstborns wanted that the B'nei Yisrael should be set free. The rest of the nation disagreed, and a civil war broke out, in which the Egyptian firstborns fought against the rest of the Egyptians, and many Egyptians were killed.

A DEEPER LOOK

Q Why do we leave pieces of chametz to be found, if the purpose of the bedikah is to find chametz that we don't know about?

A There are many reasons for this, including:

1. The halachah is that if one does not find any chametz during bedikas chametz, the next morning he should burn the item intended to hold any chametz found during the bedikah. This is so that at least **something** should be burnt to prevent one from forgetting about the obligation of performing biur chametz. Hiding pieces of chametz avoids this situation by ensuring that actual chametz will be found.

2. In the morning, we say in Kol Chamira, "All chametz... **that I have seen**... (should be hefker)." If we would not have found any chametz, this statement would be problematic. To make this statement true, we place pieces of chametz to ensure that there will actually be chametz that we "have seen."

MINHAGIM

The minhag of the Rebbeim was to wrap the pieces of chametz in paper.

They would search using a beeswax candle, a bird feather, and a wooden spoon; and as they found each piece, they would put it in a small paper bag.

After the bedikah, they would wrap the bag with the chametz, the spoon, the candle, and the feather in paper, leaving the handle of the spoon sticking out of the top of the paper, and then tighten the paper closed by wrapping a string a few times around it.

HISTORY

Hilchos Pesach was the first part of the Alter Rebbe's Shulchan Aruch to be published. The Alter Rebbe wrote these halachos while he was in Mezritch, studying under the guidance of the Maggid.

A DEEPER LOOK

Q Why do we hide exactly ten pieces of chametz?

A There is a reason according to Kabbalah for hiding exactly ten pieces.
It is also hinted in the Gemara in Pesachim where it discusses a case where a person left ten pieces of chametz lying around his house, and found only nine while searching for them.

DID YOU KNOW?

The basic obligation of bedikas chametz is to **search** for chametz; even if you don't find anything, you have still fulfilled the mitzvah.

MINHAGIM

שַׁבָּת הַגָּדוֹל

Q Are there any special minhagim associated with Shabbos Hagadol?

A After Minchah on Shabbos Hagadol, we say the section of Maggid beginning with עֲבָדִים הָיִינוּ and concluding with לְכַפֵּר עַל כָּל עֲוֹנוֹתֵינוּ (at the end of Dayenu).

We do this because the Shabbos before Yetzias Mitzrayim was when the miracles began.

Before starting the search, say the following
brachah while holding the lit candle:

בָּרוּךְ אַתָּה יְיָ אֱלֹהֵינוּ מֶלֶךְ הָעוֹלָם, אֲשֶׁר קִדְּשָׁנוּ בְּמִצְוֹתָיו, וְצִוָּנוּ עַל בִּעוּר חָמֵץ.

בָּרוּךְ Blessed are You, Hashem, our God, King of the world, Who made us holy with His mitzvos and commanded us regarding the removal of chametz.

וְאַחַר הַבְּדִיקָה יִזָּהֵר בֶּחָמֵץ שֶׁמְּשַׁיֵּר לְהַצְנִיעוֹ לְמָחָר לְשָׂרְפָה אוֹ לַאֲכִילָה לְשָׁמְרוֹ שֶׁלֹּא יוֹלִיכוּהוּ אַנָה וַאֲנָה שֶׁלֹּא יִתְפָּרֵר וְיִתְגָּרֵר מִמֶּנּוּ עַל יְדֵי תִּינוֹקוֹת אוֹ עַכְבָּרִים. וְגַם צָרִיךְ לְבַטֵּל אַחַר הַבְּדִיקָה וְיֹאמַר:

After the search, wrap the paper bag, candle, feather, and spoon in a paper. Tie it well, with the spoon handle sticking out. Nullify the chametz that may have been overlooked by saying the following (in a language that you understand):

כָּל חֲמִירָא וַחֲמִיעָא דְּאִכָּא בִרְשׁוּתִי, דְּלָא חֲמִתֵּיהּ וּדְלָא בַעַרְתֵּיהּ וּדְלָא יְדַעְנָא לֵיהּ, לִבָּטֵל וְלֶהֱוֵי הֶפְקֵר כְּעַפְרָא דְּאַרְעָא.

כָּל All chametz and anything that contains chametz that is in my possession, which I did not see, remove, or know about, should be nullified and ownerless like the dust of the earth.

Store the bag of chametz (as well as any chametz that will be eaten in the morning) out of the reach of children or animals who may scatter it.

NUSACH

Q Why is Kol Chamira in Aramaic?

A It was originally written in Lashon Hakodesh. However, in the times of the Geonim, (about 1000-1400 years ago) many people did not understand Lashon Hakodesh, so the Geonim decided that it be said in the common language at that time, Aramaic. That way, everyone would be able to understand the words.

But, as mentioned above, it is most important to say it in a language that you understand.

WORD POWER

Q Why do we say in the brachah before searching for the chametz, "עַל בִּעוּר חָמֵץ," which means "regarding the removal of chametz," if we're not going to burn the chametz until the next morning?

A When we say Kol Chamira after the search, we are making our chametz hefker (ownerless). This is also considered biur chametz, since it removes chametz from our possession, just as burning does.

In addition, no brachah will be said the following day when the chametz is burned. The brachah said at this point is also for the burning of chametz the next morning.

MINHAGIM

The Zohar says that eating chametz on Pesach is like serving avodah zarah.

The Arizal said that if you are very careful to stay away from the tiniest amount of chametz during Pesach, you will not do any accidental aveiros throughout the entire year.

STORY

The Alter Rebbe first went to Mezritch in 5524 (1764). When he returned home, on the 13th of Nissan 5525 (1765), he did not eat the whole day because he was so focused on preparing for bedikas chametz; he wanted to apply all that he learned from the Maggid regarding this mitzvah. His bedikas chametz lasted the entire night even though his residence had only one room!

DID YOU KNOW?

One should begin the search in the room closest to the place where the brachah "עַל בְּעוּר חָמֵץ" was made, in order to avoid a hefsek (interruption) between saying the brachah and performing the mitzvah.

NUSACH

Q Why do we add the words (like the dust) "of the earth;" wouldn't it be enough to say that the chametz is as worthless as dust?

A Gold can also be crushed into "dust." We want to emphasize that chametz is as worthless as the dust of the earth, and not gold dust!

בִּיעוּר חָמֵץ

בְּיוֹם י״ד בְּשָׁעָה ה׳ יַעֲשֶׂה לוֹ מְדוּרָה בִּפְנֵי עַצְמוֹ וְיִשְׂרְפֵנוּ וִיבַטְלֶנוּ וּבְבִטּוּל הַיוֹם יֹאמַר:

On the fourteenth of Nissan, chametz may be eaten only until the end of the fourth "hour" (check your local Jewish calendar for exact times). In the fifth "hour," burn any remaining chametz, including the ten pieces.

Say the following (in a language that you understand) to nullify any remaining chametz:

כָּל חֲמִירָא וַחֲמִיעָא דְאִכָּא בִרְשׁוּתִי, דַּחֲזִיתֵיהּ וּדְלָא חֲזִיתֵיהּ, דַּחֲמִיתֵיהּ וּדְלָא חֲמִיתֵיהּ, דְּבִעַרְתֵּיהּ וּדְלָא בִעַרְתֵּיהּ, לִבָּטֵל וְלֶהֱוֵי הֶפְקֵר כְּעַפְרָא דְאַרְעָא.

וְיֵשׁ לִשְׂרוֹף עֲשָׂרָה פְּתִיתִין וּבְשָׁעַת שְׂרֵפַת הֶחָמֵץ יֹאמַר זֶה:

Continue with the following tefillah:

יְהִי רָצוֹן מִלְפָנֶיךָ יְיָ אֱלֹהֵינוּ וֵאלֹהֵי אֲבוֹתֵינוּ, כְּשֵׁם שֶׁאֲנִי מְבַעֵר חָמֵץ מִבֵּיתִי וּמֵרְשׁוּתִי, כַּךְ תְּבַעֵר אֶת כָּל הַחִיצוֹנִים, וְאֶת רוּחַ הַטֻּמְאָה תַּעֲבִיר מִן הָאָרֶץ, וְאֶת יִצְרֵנוּ הָרַע תַּעֲבִירֵהוּ מֵאִתָּנוּ, וְתִתֶּן לָנוּ לֵב בָּשָׂר לְעָבְדְּךָ בֶּאֱמֶת, וְכָל סִטְרָא אָחֳרָא וְכָל הַקְּלִפּוֹת וְכָל הָרִשְׁעָה בְּעָשָׁן תִּכְלֶה, וְתַעֲבִיר מֶמְשֶׁלֶת זָדוֹן מִן הָאָרֶץ, וְכָל הַמְעִיקִים לַשְּׁכִינָה תְּבַעֲרֵם בְּרוּחַ בָּעֵר וּבְרוּחַ מִשְׁפָּט כְּשֵׁם שֶׁבִּעַרְתָּ אֶת מִצְרַיִם וְאֶת אֱלֹהֵיהֶם בַּיָמִים הָהֵם בִּזְמַן הַזֶּה, אָמֵן סֶלָה.

During the burning of the chametz in the morning, one should clean out one's pockets to empty any chametz crumbs that may have settled there.

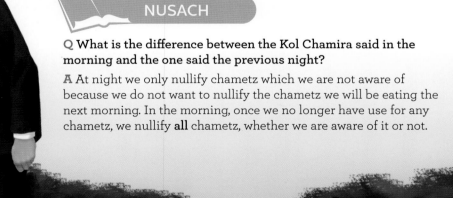

NUSACH

Q What is the difference between the Kol Chamira said in the morning and the one said the previous night?

A At night we only nullify chametz which we are not aware of because we do not want to nullify the chametz we will be eating the next morning. In the morning, once we no longer have use for any chametz, we nullify **all** chametz, whether we are aware of it or not.

BURNING THE CHAMETZ

כָּל All chametz and anything that contains **chametz that is in my possession, whether I saw it** during bedikas chametz **or not, whether I have** ever **noticed it or not, whether I removed it or not, should be nullified and ownerless like the dust of the earth.**

יְהִי **May it be Your will, Hashem, our God and the God of our fathers,** that just as I am destroying chametz from my house and from my possession, so too **should You destroy all the outside forces** that oppose kedushah, **remove the spirit of tumah from the world, remove the yetzer hara from us, and give us a heart of flesh** (that feels kedushah, not like a heart of stone that feels nothing) **to serve You truthfully. Destroy all the sitra achara, all the kelipos, and all the wickedness in smoke. Remove the rule of evil from the land. Destroy all those who oppose the Shechinah with a spirit of destruction and justice, just as You destroyed the Egyptians and their gods in those days, at this time. Amen, selah.**

סֵדֶר קָרְבַּן פֶּסַח

וּנְשַׁלְּמָה פָרִים שְׂפָתֵינוּ וּתְפִלַּת מִנְחָה הִיא בִּמְקוֹם מִנְחָה תָּמִיד שֶׁל בֵּין הָעַרְבַּיִם וּבִזְמַן שֶׁבֵּית הַמִּקְדָּשׁ הָיָה קַיָּם הָיָה הַפֶּסַח נִשְׁחָט אַחַר תָּמִיד שֶׁל בֵּין הָעַרְבַּיִם כֵּן רָאוּי לַעֲסוֹק בְּסֵדֶר קָרְבַּן פֶּסַח אַחַר תְּפִלַּת הַמִּנְחָה וְיֹאמַר זֶה:

"We offer the words of our lips in place of the korbanos." The tefillah of Minchah takes the place of the Korban Tamid of the afternoon; and in the time of the Beis Hamikdash, the Korban Pesach was offered after the Korban Tamid of the afternoon. Therefore, it is appropriate to study the order of the Korban Pesach after Minchah.

On Erev Pesach after Minchah, say the following:

קָרְבַּן פֶּסַח מֵבִיא מִן הַכְּבָשִׂים אוֹ מִן הָעִזִּים זָכָר בֶּן שָׁנָה, וְשׁוֹחֲטוֹ בָּעֲזָרָה בְּכָל מָקוֹם, אַחַר חֲצוֹת אַרְבָּעָה עָשָׂר דַּוְקָא, וְאַחַר שְׁחִיטַת תָּמִיד שֶׁל בֵּין הָעַרְבַּיִם, וְאַחַר הֲטָבַת נֵרוֹת שֶׁל בֵּין הָעַרְבַּיִם. וְאֵין שׁוֹחֲטִין אֶת הַפֶּסַח עַל הֶחָמֵץ. וְאִם שָׁחַט קוֹדֶם לַתָּמִיד, כָּשֵׁר, וּבִלְבַד שֶׁיְּהֵא אַחֵר מְמָרֵס בְּדַם הַפֶּסַח כְּדֵי שֶׁלֹּא יִקְרַשׁ עַד שֶׁיִּזְרְקוּ דַּם הַתָּמִיד, וְאַחַר כָּךְ יִזְרְקוּ דַּם הַפֶּסַח זְרִיקָה אַחַת כְּנֶגֶד הַיְסוֹד.

וְכֵיצַד עוֹשִׂין? שָׁחַט הַשּׁוֹחֵט, וְקִבֵּל הַכֹּהֵן הָרִאשׁוֹן שֶׁבְּרֹאשׁ הַשּׁוּרָה וְנָתַן לַחֲבֵרוֹ, וַחֲבֵרוֹ לַחֲבֵרוֹ, וְהַכֹּהֵן הַקָּרוֹב אֵצֶל הַמִּזְבֵּחַ זוֹרְקוֹ זְרִיקָה אַחַת כְּנֶגֶד הַיְסוֹד, וְחוֹזֵר הַכְּלִי רֵיקָן לַחֲבֵרוֹ, וַחֲבֵרוֹ לַחֲבֵרוֹ, וּמְקַבֵּל כְּלִי הַמָּלֵא תְּחִלָּה וְאַחַר כָּךְ מַחֲזִיר הָרֵיקָן. וְהָיוּ שׁוּרוֹת שֶׁל בָּזִיכֵי כֶסֶף וְשׁוּרוֹת שֶׁל בָּזִיכֵי זָהָב. וְלֹא הָיוּ לַבָּזִיכִין שׁוּלַיִם, שֶׁמָּא יַנִּיחֵם וְיִקְרַשׁ הַדָּם.

אַחַר כָּךְ תּוֹלִין אֶת הַפֶּסַח וּמַפְשִׁיטִין אוֹתוֹ כֻּלּוֹ, וְקוֹרְעִין אוֹתוֹ, וּמְמַחִין אֶת קְרָבָיו עַד שֶׁיֵּצֵא הַפֶּרֶשׁ, וּמוֹצִיאִין אֶת הָאֵימוּרִים, וְהֵם: הַחֵלֶב שֶׁעַל הַקֶּרֶב, וְיוֹתֶרֶת הַכָּבֵד, וּשְׁתֵּי כְלָיוֹת וְהַחֵלֶב שֶׁעֲלֵיהֶן, וְהָאַלְיָה לְעֻמַּת הֶעָצֶה, וְנוֹתְנָם בִּכְלִי שָׁרֵת, וּמוֹלְחָם וּמַקְטִירָם הַכֹּהֵן עַל גַּבֵּי הַמִּזְבֵּחַ כָּל אֶחָד לְבַדּוֹ.

THE ORDER OF THE KORBAN PESACH

קָרְבָּן **The Korban Pesach is brought from male lambs or goats** which are less than **a year old, and** can be **shechted anywhere in the Azarah after chatzos of the fourteenth** of Nissan (Erev Pesach). It must be done **after the shechting of the afternoon Korban Tamid and after the afternoon cleaning of the cups** of the menorah. **One should not shecht the** Korban **Pesach while he** still **has chametz in his possession. If he shechted** the Korban Pesach **before the Korban Tamid** of the afternoon, the Korban Pesach **is** still **kosher, as long as someone stirs the blood of the** Korban **Pesach so that it** will remain liquid and **not harden by** the time **the blood of the** Korban **Tamid is poured** on the Mizbei'ach. **After** pouring the blood of the Korban Tamid, **the blood of the Korban Pesach is poured once toward the base** of the Mizbei'ach.

How is the offering of the Korban Pesach **performed?**

The Kohanim would form lines across the Azarah between each shechitah station and the Mizbei'ach, and they would hold vessels with which to pass the blood down the line. **The shochet would** then **shecht the korban, and the Kohen** standing **at the head of the line would catch** the blood in his vessel **and pass it to his friend. His friend** would then pass the vessel full of blood **to his friend** next in line, and so on, until the vessel would reach **the Kohen standing closest to the Mizbei'ach, who would pour it once toward the base** of the Mizbei'ach. He would pass **the empty vessel back to his friend, who would** pass it on **to his friend** until it was returned to the head of the line. If a Kohen was holding an empty vessel heading back up the line to be reused, and the Kohen ahead of him wanted to pass him a full vessel to be passed down the line and poured on the Mizbei'ach, he would **first take the full vessel** from his friend **and** only **then pass** him **the empty** vessel. This procedure follows the rule that one may not "pass by" and delay an available mitzvah. To beautify the occasion, all the vessels in each line were of the same material; **there were lines** in which all **of** the Kohanim held **silver vessels and lines** in which all **of** the Kohanim held **gold vessels. The vessels did not have flat bottoms in case** the Kohanim **would put them down and** forget about them, **causing the blood to thicken.** If this happened, the blood would be unfit to pour on the Mizbei'ach.

Afterwards, the Korban **Pesach would be hung** on iron hooks, **and** the Kohanim **would remove all the skin and tear it** open. **They would clean out the insides until the waste was removed, and** then **they would take out the parts** of the korban which were going to be offered on the Mizbei'ach. **These** parts **are: The fat that is on the intestines, a lobe of the liver, the two kidneys with the fat on them, and the tail** up to **the backbone above** the kidneys. The parts **would be placed in a bowl** which was used especially for the **service** in the Beis Hamikdash. **The Kohen would salt each individual part and burn it on the Mizbei'ach.**

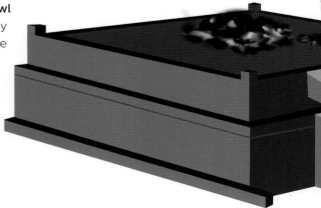

וְהַשְּׁחִיטָה וְהַזְּרִיקָה וּמִחוּי קְרָבָיו וְהֶקְטֵר חֲלָבָיו דּוֹחִין אֶת הַשַּׁבָּת, וּשְׁאָר עִנְיָנָיו אֵינָם דּוֹחִין אֶת הַשַּׁבָּת. וְכֵן אֵין מוֹלִיכִין אֶת הַפֶּסַח לַבַּיִת כְּשֶׁחָל בְּשַׁבָּת, אֶלָּא כַּת הָאַחַת הֵם מִתְעַכְּבִים עִם פִּסְחֵיהֶם בְּהַר הַבַּיִת, וְהַכַּת הַשְּׁנִיָּה יוֹשֶׁבֶת לָהּ בַּחֵיל, וְהַשְּׁלִישִׁית בִּמְקוֹמָהּ עוֹמֶדֶת. חָשְׁכָה, יָצְאוּ וְצָלוּ פִּסְחֵיהֶם.

בִּשְׁלֹשָׁה כִּתּוֹת הַפֶּסַח נִשְׁחָט, וְאֵין כַּת פְּחוּתָה מִשְּׁלֹשִׁים אֲנָשִׁים. נִכְנְסָה כַּת הָרִאשׁוֹנָה, נִתְמַלְּאָה הָעֲזָרָה, נוֹעֲלִין אוֹתָהּ. וּבְעוֹד שֶׁהֵם שׁוֹחֲטִין וּמַקְרִיבִין אֶת הָאֵימוּרִים, קוֹרְאִין אֶת הַהַלֵּל. אִם גָּמְרוּ אוֹתוֹ קֹדֶם שֶׁיַּקְרִיבוּ כֻלָּם, שׁוֹנִים אוֹתוֹ, וְאִם שָׁנוּ יְשַׁלֵּשׁוּ. עַל כָּל קְרִיאָה תּוֹקְעִין שָׁלֹשׁ תְּקִיעוֹת. תְּקִיעָה תְּרוּעָה תְּקִיעָה.

גָּמְרוּ לְהַקְרִיב, פּוֹתְחִין הָעֲזָרָה. יָצְאָה כַּת רִאשׁוֹנָה, נִכְנְסָה כַּת שְׁנִיָּה, נוֹעֲלִין דַּלְתוֹת הָעֲזָרָה. גָּמְרוּ, פּוֹתְחִין, יָצְאָה כַּת שְׁנִיָּה, נִכְנְסָה כַּת שְׁלִישִׁית, וּמַעֲשֵׂה כֻלָּן שָׁוִין.

וְאַחַר שֶׁיָּצְאוּ כֻלָּן רוֹחֲצִין הָעֲזָרָה, וַאֲפִילוּ בְּשַׁבָּת, מִפְּנֵי לִכְלוּךְ הַדָּם שֶׁהָיָה בָהּ. וְכֵיצַד הָיְתָה הָרְחִיצָה? אַמַּת הַמַּיִם הָיְתָה עוֹבֶרֶת בָּעֲזָרָה, וְהָיָה לָהּ מָקוֹם לָצֵאת מִמֶּנָּה, וּכְשֶׁרוֹצִין לְהָדִיחַ אֶת הָרִצְפָּה, סוֹתְמִין מְקוֹם יְצִיאָתָהּ, וְהִיא מִתְמַלֵּאת עַל כָּל גְּדוֹתֶיהָ מִפֹּה וּמִפֹּה, עַד שֶׁהַמַּיִם עוֹלִים וְצָפִים מִכָּאן וּמִכָּאן, וּמְקַבֵּץ אֵלֶיהָ כָּל דָּם וְכָל לִכְלוּךְ שֶׁהָיָה בָעֲזָרָה. וְאַחַר כָּךְ פּוֹתְחִין מְקוֹם יְצִיאָתָהּ, וְהַכֹּל יוֹצֵא עַד שֶׁנִּשְׁאָר הָרִצְפָּה מְנֻקָּה וּמְשֻׁפָּה. זֶהוּ כְּבוֹד הַבַּיִת.

וְאִם הַפֶּסַח נִמְצָא טְרֵפָה, לֹא עָלָה לוֹ עַד שֶׁמֵּבִיא אַחֵר.

זֶה הָעִנְיָן בְּקִצּוּר גָּדוֹל. וְצָרִיךְ הָאָדָם הַיָּרֵא וְחָרֵד עַל דְּבַר ה' לִקְרוֹת אוֹתוֹ בִּזְמַנּוֹ שֶׁתַּעֲלֶה קְרִיאָתוֹ בִּמְקוֹם הַקְרָבָתוֹ וְיִדְאַג עַל חֻרְבַּן הַבַּיִת וְיִתְחַנַּן לִפְנֵי ה' בּוֹרֵא עוֹלָם שֶׁיִּבְנֶה אוֹתוֹ בִּמְהֵרָה בְיָמֵינוּ אָמֵן.

This is a very brief description of the order of the Korban Pesach. A God-fearing person should say it in its proper time, so that its recital should be regarded as being in place of offering the Korban Pesach. One should be troubled about the destruction of the Beis Hamikdash, and plead before Hashem, the Creator of the world, that He rebuild it speedily in our days, Amen.

Shechting the Korban Pesach, **pouring** the blood on the Mizbei'ach, **cleaning the** animal's **insides, and burning its fat** on the Mizbei'ach, all **push aside** the issur of melachah on **Shabbos. However,** everything **else connected** to the Korban Pesach, such as roasting it and rinsing the intestines, **does not push aside** the issur of melachah on **Shabbos.** Also, if the fourteenth of Nissan falls out **on Shabbos, the** Korbanos Pesach are not allowed **to be carried home. Rather, the first group** of people (see next paragraph) leaves the Azarah and **waits with their** Korbanos Pesach on the Har Habayis, the **second group sits** and waits with their Korbanos Pesach **in** the area just outside the Azarah called **the "Cheil," and the third** group **stays where it is** – in the Azarah. **When it becomes dark** and Shabbos ends, they all go to their homes **and roast their** Korbanos **Pesach.**

The Korban **Pesach would be shechted in three groups, each group** consisting of **no less than thirty men. The first group would enter, fill** up **the Azarah,** and then the Kohanim **would close the doors** to the Azarah. **While** the Kohanim **were** busy **shechting** the Korban Pesach **and offering its parts** on the Mizbei'ach, **the** Levi'im **would say Hallel. If** the Levi'im **finished** saying the entire Hallel **before** the Kohanim **finished offering all** the korbanos, **they would repeat** Hallel a second time. **If the** Kohanim had not finished the avodah by the time the Levi'im finished **repeating Hallel** a second time, **they would repeat it a third time. Each** time Hallel was **said,** the Kohanim **would blow** the following **three sounds** with the trumpets: tekiah, teruah and **tekiah.**

When the Kohanim **finished offering** the korbanos, **they would open** the doors to **the Azarah** and **the first group would leave;** whereupon, **the second group would enter, and they would close the doors to the Azarah** again. When **the Kohanim finished** offering the korbanos of the second group, **they would open** the doors, **the second group would leave,** and **the third group would enter. The procedure of each group was the same.**

After all the groups had left, **the** Kohanim **would wash** the floor of **the Azarah because it had become filthy from the blood** of the korbanos, **even** if it was **Shabbos. How was the washing of the Azarah done?** There was **a water channel that ran through the Azarah,** which would flow out **through an exit** at the Sha'ar Hamayim. **When they wanted to wash the floor** of the Azarah, **they would block the exit,** causing the water level to rise and **fill the** channel **to its brim on both sides, until it would overflow and flood** the floor **on both sides** of the channel. The water would **gather all the blood and dirt on** the floor of **the Azarah into** the channel. **They would then open the exit, and all** the blood and dirt **would flow out** of the Azarah along with the water, **until the floor was** completely **clean and smooth. This** cleaning **is** done **to honor the Beis Hamikdash.**

If the animal brought for the Korban **Pesach was found to be treif,** the person bringing the korban **would not have fulfilled** his obligation **until he brings another** one.

סֵדֶר עֵירוּב תַּבְשִׁילִין

- When the first two days of Pesach occur on Thursday and Friday, one should make an "eruv tavshilin" on Wednesday. The eruv tavshilin permits one to prepare food on the second day of Yom Tov for Shabbos, which is otherwise forbidden. The eruv consists of taking a matzah and a substantial cooked food designated for Shabbos (such as meat, fish, or an egg) and saying the brachah and statement below.

- It is customary, if possible, to appoint an adult male to act as a "shliach" through whom one grants a share in one's eruv to the entire community. One who does not have a "shliach" skips the boxed section below:

- After an eruv has been made, cooking food on Friday for Shabbos (but not on Thursday for Friday or Shabbos) is permitted. One must, however, cook this food well before nightfall, so that it would be possible for one to theoretically benefit from the food on the Friday of Yom Tov, so one is not cooking only for Shabbos. The food designated for the eruv must be saved until all the tasks necessary for Shabbos have been completed.

- It is customary to use an entire matzah for the eruv, which is then used on Shabbos as one of the two lechem mishneh on Friday night and Shabbos day and is eaten at the Seudah Shlishis (third Shabbos meal). Although each household should have its own eruv, one who forgot to make one can rely on the Rav's eruv, which is done on behalf of the entire community.

Hand the matzah and cooked food to the "shliach" and say:

אֲנִי מְזַכֶּה לְכָל מִי שֶׁרוֹצֶה לִזְכּוֹת וְלִסְמוֹךְ עַל עֵרוּב זֶה.

The "shliach" raises the food items a tefach (approximately 3 inches) and then returns them to the one making the eruv.

Hold the matzah and other food item and say the following:

בָּרוּךְ אַתָּה יְיָ, אֱלֹהֵינוּ מֶלֶךְ הָעוֹלָם, אֲשֶׁר קִדְּשָׁנוּ בְּמִצְוֹתָיו, וְצִוָּנוּ עַל מִצְוַת עֵרוּב.

The following must be said in a language that one understands:

בְּדֵין יְהֵא שָׁרֵא לָנָא לַאֲפוּיֵי וּלְבַשּׁוּלֵי וּלְאַטְמוּנֵי וּלְאַדְלוּקֵי שְׁרָגָא וּלְתַקָּנָא וּלְמֶעְבַּד כָּל צָרְכָנָא מִיּוֹמָא טָבָא לְשַׁבַּתָּא, לָנָא וּלְכָל יִשְׂרָאֵל הַדָּרִים בָּעִיר הַזֹּאת.

Put aside the food items to be eaten on Shabbos.

ERUV TAVSHILIN

אֲנִי I hereby **give** a share **in this eruv to anyone who wants to participate and depend** on it.

בָּרוּךְ **Blessed are You, Hashem, our God, King of the world, Who has made us holy with His mitzvos and commanded us** through the Chachamim **regarding the mitzvah of** making an **eruv.**

בְּדֵין **With this** eruv **it will be permitted for us to bake, to cook, to put away** food in a place that will keep it warm**, to light a candle, and to prepare and to do anything on Yom Tov that is necessary for Shabbos.** These things will be permitted **for us**—the people who are making this eruv—**and for all** B'nei Yisrael who live in this city.

סֵדֶר הַדְלָקַת הַגֵּרוֹת
CANDLE LIGHTING

On Friday evening, add the orange words.

בָּרוּךְ אַתָּה יְיָ, אֱלֹהֵינוּ מֶלֶךְ הָעוֹלָם, אֲשֶׁר קִדְּשָׁנוּ בְּמִצְוֹתָיו, וְצִוָּנוּ לְהַדְלִיק נֵר שֶׁל (שַׁבָּת וְשֶׁל) יוֹם טוֹב.

בָּרוּךְ Blessed are You, Hashem, our God, King of the world, Who made us holy with His mitzvos, and commanded us through the Chachamim **to kindle the light of** (Shabbos and) **Yom Tov.**

בָּרוּךְ אַתָּה יְיָ, אֱלֹהֵינוּ מֶלֶךְ הָעוֹלָם, שֶׁהֶחֱיָנוּ וְקִיְּמָנוּ וְהִגִּיעָנוּ לִזְמַן הַזֶּה.

בָּרוּךְ Blessed are You, Hashem, our God, King of the world, **Who has given us life, kept us** alive, **and enabled us to reach this** special **time.**

- -

- It is customary to give tzedakah before lighting Yom Tov candles.

- The Yom Tov lights are lit at least eighteen minutes before sunset. If Yom Tov is on a weekday, and one did not light before sunset, the candles should be lit from a pre-existing flame.

- Girls from the age of three should light their own candle. Married women light two candles and add an additional candle for each of their children. Where there are no women, a man lights the candles.

- After lighting the candle(s), draw your hands three times around the lights and towards your face, then place them over your eyes, and say the appropriate brachos.

- If the first night of Pesach occurs on Friday night, and one forgot to light the candles before sunset, no candles should be lit at all.

- On the second night of Pesach, or when the first night occurs on Motza'ei Shabbos, the lights are kindled after tzeis hakochavim (nightfall) from a pre-existing flame. Check your local Jewish calendar for the exact times.

סֵדֶר תִּקּוּנֵי שַׁבָּת
THE ORDER FOR FRIDAY NIGHT

When the first night of Pesach occurs on Friday night, say the following quietly upon returning home from shul:

Say each of the following four paragraphs three times:

שָׁלוֹם עֲלֵיכֶם מַלְאֲכֵי הַשָּׁרֵת מַלְאֲכֵי עֶלְיוֹן
מִמֶּלֶךְ מַלְכֵי הַמְּלָכִים הַקָּדוֹשׁ בָּרוּךְ הוּא.

בּוֹאֲכֶם לְשָׁלוֹם מַלְאֲכֵי הַשָּׁלוֹם מַלְאֲכֵי עֶלְיוֹן
מִמֶּלֶךְ מַלְכֵי הַמְּלָכִים הַקָּדוֹשׁ בָּרוּךְ הוּא.

בָּרְכוּנִי לְשָׁלוֹם מַלְאֲכֵי הַשָּׁלוֹם מַלְאֲכֵי עֶלְיוֹן
מִמֶּלֶךְ מַלְכֵי הַמְּלָכִים הַקָּדוֹשׁ בָּרוּךְ הוּא.

צֵאתְכֶם לְשָׁלוֹם מַלְאֲכֵי הַשָּׁלוֹם מַלְאֲכֵי עֶלְיוֹן
מִמֶּלֶךְ מַלְכֵי הַמְּלָכִים הַקָּדוֹשׁ בָּרוּךְ הוּא.

כִּי מַלְאָכָיו יְצַוֶּה לָּךְ, לִשְׁמָרְךָ בְּכָל דְּרָכֶיךָ.
יְיָ יִשְׁמָר צֵאתְךָ וּבוֹאֶךָ, מֵעַתָּה וְעַד עוֹלָם.

אֵשֶׁת חַיִל מִי יִמְצָא, וְרָחֹק מִפְּנִינִים מִכְרָהּ. בָּטַח בָּהּ לֵב בַּעְלָהּ, וְשָׁלָל לֹא יֶחְסָר. גְּמָלַתְהוּ טוֹב וְלֹא רָע, כֹּל יְמֵי חַיֶּיהָ. דָּרְשָׁה צֶמֶר וּפִשְׁתִּים, וַתַּעַשׂ בְּחֵפֶץ כַּפֶּיהָ. הָיְתָה כָּאֳנִיּוֹת סוֹחֵר, מִמֶּרְחָק תָּבִיא לַחְמָהּ. וַתָּקָם בְּעוֹד לַיְלָה, וַתִּתֵּן טֶרֶף לְבֵיתָהּ, וְחֹק לְנַעֲרֹתֶיהָ. זָמְמָה שָׂדֶה וַתִּקָּחֵהוּ, מִפְּרִי כַפֶּיהָ נָטְעָה כָּרֶם. חָגְרָה בְעוֹז מָתְנֶיהָ, וַתְּאַמֵּץ זְרוֹעֹתֶיהָ. טָעֲמָה כִּי טוֹב סַחְרָהּ, לֹא יִכְבֶּה בַלַּיְלָה נֵרָהּ. יָדֶיהָ שִׁלְחָה בַכִּישׁוֹר, וְכַפֶּיהָ תָּמְכוּ פָלֶךְ.

שָׁלוֹם **Peace** should be **upon you, angels who serve Hashem, messengers of** Hashem, **high** above, angels **of** Hashem, the **Supreme King of** all **kings, the Holy One, blessed be He.**

בּוֹאֲכֶם **May your arrival** to our home **be in peace, angels of peace, messengers of** Hashem, **high** above, angels **of** Hashem, the **Supreme King of** all **kings, the Holy One, blessed be He.**

בָּרְכוּנִי **Bless me with peace, angels of peace, messengers of** Hashem, **high** above, angels **of** Hashem, the **Supreme King of** all **kings, the Holy One, blessed be He.**

צֵאתְכֶם **May your departure** from our home **be in peace, angels of peace, messengers of** Hashem, **high** above, angels **of** Hashem, the **Supreme King of** all **kings, the Holy One, blessed be He.**

Hashem will **command His angels on your behalf, to guard you in all your ways. Hashem will guard your departure and your arrival** when traveling, **from now and forever.**

אֵשֶׁת **Who can find a wife of excellence;** a wife who has all the following qualities? **Her value is far** greater **than the most precious jewels. When her husband** is away, his **heart trusts in her.** He trusts that she will take care of everything. Since he has nothing to worry about, he can do his work, **and he will not miss** out on **any** business **gains. All the days of her life, she treats him** well; she does **good** things for him, **and never bad** things. **She** goes out to **search for wool and flax** to sew clothing, **and she does** it **willingly, with her** own **hands. She is like the ships** that carry **merchandise** from far away, because **she brings her food from far away. She gets up while it is still nighttime,** before the sun rises, **and gives food to her household and** divides **jobs for her maids. She considers** buying a field because of its great value, **and** then **buys it** without delay. **From the earnings** which she receives for the work **of her hands, she plants a vineyard. She puts on her** clothing **with strength, and flexes her arms** for work. When **she realizes that her work is good** and she can benefit from it, she will stay up all night to work; **her candle will not go out** all **night. She puts her hands on a spindle** (a tool which spins wool into a thread) **and her palms hold onto a distaff** (a tool which holds wool in place while it is being spun). With these tools she makes clothing for her household. **She holds out her hand** and gives money **to the**

כַּפָּהּ פָּרְשָׂה לֶעָנִי, וְיָדֶיהָ שִׁלְּחָה לָאֶבְיוֹן. לֹא תִירָא לְבֵיתָהּ מִשָּׁלֶג, כִּי כָל בֵּיתָהּ לָבֻשׁ שָׁנִים. מַרְבַדִּים עָשְׂתָה לָּהּ, שֵׁשׁ וְאַרְגָּמָן לְבוּשָׁהּ. נוֹדָע בַּשְּׁעָרִים בַּעְלָהּ, בְּשִׁבְתּוֹ עִם זִקְנֵי אָרֶץ. סָדִין עָשְׂתָה וַתִּמְכֹּר, וַחֲגוֹר נָתְנָה לַכְּנַעֲנִי. עֹז וְהָדָר לְבוּשָׁהּ, וַתִּשְׂחַק לְיוֹם אַחֲרוֹן. פִּיהָ פָּתְחָה בְחָכְמָה, וְתוֹרַת חֶסֶד עַל לְשׁוֹנָהּ. צוֹפִיָּה הֲלִיכוֹת בֵּיתָהּ, וְלֶחֶם עַצְלוּת לֹא תֹאכֵל. קָמוּ בָנֶיהָ וַיְאַשְּׁרוּהָ, בַּעְלָהּ וַיְהַלְלָהּ. רַבּוֹת בָּנוֹת עָשׂוּ חָיִל, וְאַתְּ עָלִית עַל כֻּלָּנָה. שֶׁקֶר הַחֵן וְהֶבֶל הַיֹּפִי, אִשָּׁה יִרְאַת יְיָ הִיא תִתְהַלָּל. תְּנוּ לָהּ מִפְּרִי יָדֶיהָ, וִיהַלְלוּהָ בַשְּׁעָרִים מַעֲשֶׂיהָ.

מִזְמוֹר לְדָוִד, יְיָ רֹעִי לֹא אֶחְסָר. בִּנְאוֹת דֶּשֶׁא יַרְבִּיצֵנִי, עַל מֵי מְנֻחוֹת יְנַהֲלֵנִי. נַפְשִׁי יְשׁוֹבֵב, יַנְחֵנִי בְמַעְגְּלֵי צֶדֶק לְמַעַן שְׁמוֹ. גַּם כִּי אֵלֵךְ בְּגֵיא צַלְמָוֶת לֹא אִירָא רָע, כִּי אַתָּה עִמָּדִי, שִׁבְטְךָ וּמִשְׁעַנְתֶּךָ הֵמָּה יְנַחֲמֻנִי. תַּעֲרֹךְ לְפָנַי שֻׁלְחָן נֶגֶד צֹרְרָי, דִּשַּׁנְתָּ בַשֶּׁמֶן רֹאשִׁי, כּוֹסִי רְוָיָה. אַךְ טוֹב וָחֶסֶד יִרְדְּפוּנִי כָּל יְמֵי חַיָּי, וְשַׁבְתִּי בְּבֵית יְיָ לְאֹרֶךְ יָמִים.

דָּא הִיא סְעוּדָתָא דַחֲקַל תַּפּוּחִין קַדִּישִׁין.

אַתְקִינוּ סְעוּדָתָא דִמְהֵימְנוּתָא שְׁלֵמָתָא חֶדְוָתָא דְמַלְכָּא קַדִּישָׁא. אַתְקִינוּ סְעוּדָתָא דְמַלְכָּא, דָּא הִיא סְעוּדָתָא דַחֲקַל תַּפּוּחִין קַדִּישִׁין, וּזְעֵיר אַנְפִּין וְעַתִּיקָא קַדִּישָׁא אַתְיָן לְסַעֲדָא בַּהֲדָהּ.

poor, and extends her hands to give money **to poor** people who are too embarrassed to ask for it. **She is not afraid that her household** will be cold **from snow** in the winter, **because her entire household is wearing** warm, **colored clothing. She makes herself beautiful material; she** wears beautiful **clothing** made **of fine linen and purple** wool. Since she makes beautiful clothing for her household, **her husband is well-known** among the important people who gather **at the gates; when he sits with the elders of the land,** they know who he is. **She** also **makes bed-linens** for others **and sells them; she supplies belts to merchants. She** wears **beautiful and strong clothing** that last a long time **and** she is certain that she **will be happy in** her **last days,** when she becomes old. **She opens her mouth with wisdom, and lessons of kindness are** always **on her tongue. She watches the conduct of her household;** she makes sure that her family is following the path of Torah. **She does not** take a long time to **eat** her **bread; she is not lazy. Her children get up and praise her. Her husband praises her** with the following praise: There are **many daughters** who **have done excellent things, but you are** far **better than all of them. Charm is misleading, and beauty is nothing** to be praised for, but **a woman who fears Hashem is** worthy of being **praised.** The father tells his children to **give praise to** their mother **for her accomplishments.** The important people who sit **at the gates will praise her** for everything **she has done.**

מִזְמוֹר The following **song** was composed **by Dovid** Hamelech: **Hashem is my shepherd** Who takes care of me. I am sure that **I will not lack anything. He lies me down in** comfortable **green grass,** just like a shepherd with his sheep, and **He leads me** peacefully, as if I am walking **along calm waters. He** always **refreshes my soul. He directs me** along **the path of righteousness** in order **to** bring honor to **His name. Even when I walk in** a dangerous place, like **the valley of the shadow of death, I will not be afraid** that **bad** things will happen **because You are with me. Your** help and kindness are like a walking **stick and** support **staff** which protect me and **comfort me.** Hashem will **set up a table for me in front of my enemies,** filled with all the best things, and they will see that I have become successful. **You have anointed me with oil** to make me king, and **my cup is full** with everything I need. Even though You always save me from bad things, I ask and hope that from now on **only good and kindness will follow me all the days of my life, and** that **I will sit in the House of Hashem,** the Beis Hamikdash, **for** many **long years.**

אֲדַ **This is the meal** of Hashem's Shechinah, which is called **the holy Chakal Tapuchin.**

אַתְקִינוּ **Prepare the meal of perfect faith,** which brings **happiness** to Hashem, **the holy King. Prepare the meal of the King.** This is the meal of Hashem's Shechinah, which is called **the holy Chakal Tapuchin.** Two other levels of the Shechinah—Z'eir Anpin and Atika Kadisha— **come to join** Chakal Tapuchin **at the meal.**

סֵדֶר הַגָּדָה

יְסַדֵּר עַל שֻׁלְחָנוֹ קְעָרָה בְּג' מַצוֹת מֻנָּחִים זֶה עַל זֶה הַיִּשְׂרָאֵל וְעָלָיו הַלֵּוִי וְעָלָיו הַכֹּהֵן וְעָלָיו לְיָמִין הַזְּרוֹעַ וּכְנֶגְדּוֹ לִשְׂמֹאל הַבֵּיצָה תַּחְתֵּיהֶם בָּאֶמְצַע הַמָּרוֹר וְתַחַת הַזְּרוֹעַ הַחֲרֹסֶת וּכְנֶגְדּוֹ תַּחַת הַבֵּיצָה הַכַּרְפַּס וְתַחַת הַמָּרוֹר הַחֲזֶרֶת שֶׁעוֹשִׂין כּוֹרֵךְ:

The Seder should begin soon after returning home from shul, but not before tzeis hakochavim (nightfall).

It is customary to prepare the kaarah after tzeis hakochavim. On the second night, the table should not be set before tzeis hakochavim.

Organize the kaarah in the following order:

Three whole matzos are placed on a tray or large plate, with a cloth (or napkin) between each matzah. Place the first matzah in the lowest "compartment." This will be the "Yisrael" matzah. Place another (the "Levi" matzah) above it, and another matzah above these (the "Kohen" matzah).

1 Place a roasted bird's-neck-bone on top of the matzos, on the upper right side. One should not eat from the zero'a. Minhag Chabad is to remove most of the meat from the bone.

2 Place a hard-boiled egg on the upper left side.

3 Place a kezayis of bitter herbs in the center. It is the minhag to use romaine lettuce and horseradish for marror.

4 Place charoses—a mixture of apples, nuts, pears on the lower right side, under the zero'a. (Add wine before eating the marror.)

5 Place some raw onion (or a boiled potato) on the lower left side, under the egg.

6 Place a kezayis of bitter herbs in the center, under the marror. It is the minhag to use romaine lettuce and horseradish for chazeres.

WORD POWER

Q Why is it called the "Haggadah?"

A Some say that the name "Haggadah" comes from the words "וְהִגַּדְתָּ לְבִנְךָ" — "and you shall tell your son," found in the passuk that commands us to tell the story of Yetzias Mitzrayim.

Others say that it means praise and thanks—as in the passuk הִגַּדְתִּי הַיּוֹם, said when bringing bikkurim, in which we thank Hashem for the produce He gave us—because in the Haggadah we thank Hashem for taking us out of Egypt.

HISTORY

Q Why do we use three matzos on our kaarah?

A When Avraham was visited by the angels, he asked Sarah to bake matzos from three se'ah (measures) of flour. This happened on Pesach.

In addition, the matzos are a reminder of the three avos; Avraham, Yitzchak, and Yaakov.

DID YOU KNOW?

Charoses reminds us of the cement with which B'nei Yisrael worked in Mitzrayim.
It is made with fruits to which the Torah compares B'nei Yisrael, and red liquid (wine) is added, to commemorate the makkah of Dam.

A DEEPER LOOK

Q Why do we have an egg and a zero'a on the kaarah?

A The Gemara says that there must be two cooked foods on the kaarah as a reminder of the two special korbanos brought on Erev Pesach: the Korban Chagigah and the Korban Pesach.

A roasted zero'a is used to commemorate the Korban Pesach, and a hardboiled egg—which symbolizes mourning—is used nowadays to commemorate the Korban Chagigah and to remind us of the destruction of the Beis Hamikdash.

DID YOU KNOW?

Q Why isn't the zero'a eaten, unlike everything else on the kaarah?

A It is forbidden to offer a korban outside of the Beis Hamikdash. Since the zero'a is a reminder of the Korban Pesach, we do whatever possible to differentiate it from a real korban. Therefore, the zero'a is not eaten.

This is also one of the reasons why we use a chicken bone—and not a lamb's bone—as the Korban Pesach was a lamb, and why we remove as much of the meat from the bone as possible.

SEDER OF THE SEDER

Our minhag is to have the kaarah set out on the table at the beginning of the Seder, unlike others who have the minhag to bring it out only after Kiddush.

This is also apparent from the fact that the Alter Rebbe wrote the instructions for arranging the kaarah before Kiddush.

סִימָן סֵדֶר שֶׁל פֶּסַח

SIMAN OF THE PESACH SEDER

Say **Kiddush**   קַדֵּשׁ

And wash your hands   וּרְחַץ

Eat a **vegetable**   כַּרְפַּס

Break the middle matzah   יַחַץ

Tell the story of Yetzias Mitzrayim   מַגִּיד

Wash the hands   רָחְצָה

Say the **brachah of Hamotzi** on the matzah   מוֹצִיא

Say the brachah on and eating **matzah**   מַצָּה

Eat a **bitter vegetable**   מָרוֹר

Wrap together the matzah and marror   כּוֹרֵךְ

A set table for eating the Yom Tov meal   שֻׁלְחָן עוֹרֵךְ

Eat the **hidden Afikoman**   צָפוּן

Say **Birkas** Hamazon   בֵּרֵךְ

Say the second part of **Hallel**   הַלֵּל

Our Seder is **accepted favorably** by Hashem   נִרְצָה

MINHAGIM

A person should be very careful to perform the mitzvos of the Seder and say the Haggadah as established by the Chachamim. Even if some of the things we do seem unimportant, we should not think lightly of them, and must realize that everything we do has a meaning.

STORY

Generally, the Alter Rebbe did not have silverware in his home. His Chassidim once collected money and bought him a silver bowl, as well as a silver menorah. This silver bowl would be placed on the table at the Seder of the Rebbeim.

WORD POWER

Q Of all the fifteen simanim, why does only וּרְחַץ have a "וּ" before it?

A This is so that the simanim are consistent, each having two syllables.

DID YOU KNOW?

Q Why do we drink specifically *four* cups of wine?

A There are many things the number four represents, including:

1. The four terms of geulah that Hashem used to describe how He would end Galus Mitzrayim: וְהוֹצֵאתִי וְהִצַּלְתִּי וְגָאַלְתִּי וְלָקַחְתִּי. These four terms corresponded to the four decrees which Paraoh made against the Jews:

   a. Jews must work for the Egyptians.

   b. Midwives must kill all newborn Jewish males.

   c. All newborn Jewish males must be thrown into the Nile.

   d. The Jews must find the necessary straw to build bricks themselves.

2. The four letters which make up Hashem's name, י - ה - ו - ה.

STORY

The Rebbe Rashab once told the Frierdiker Rebbe:

"During the Seder—especially when the door is opened for Eliyahu Hanavi—think about being a mentsch, and then Hashem will help. Don't ask for physical things; ask for spiritual things!"

Fill your Kiddush cup to the top so that the wine overflows a little.
Then say:

אַתְקִינוּ סְעוּדָתָא דְמַלְכָּא עִלָּאָה, דָא הִיא סְעוּדָתָא דְקוּדְשָׁא בְּרִיךְ הוּא וּשְׁכִינְתֵּיה.

- Stand for Kiddush, and take the cup of wine in the right hand, pass it to the left hand, and lower it onto the palm of the right hand.

- The cup should be held three tefachim (approximately 9 in.) above the table throughout Kiddush. (Note:

This procedure is followed every time the cup is held throughout the Seder.)

- Glance at the Yom Tov candles (as on Shabbos and other Yamim Tovim), then recite Kiddush.

כְּשֶׁחָל יוֹם טוֹב בְּשַׁבָּת תְּחִלָּה אוֹמְרִים "יוֹם הַשִּׁשִּׁי":
On a Friday night, begin here.

יוֹם הַשִּׁשִּׁי. וַיְכֻלּוּ הַשָּׁמַיִם וְהָאָרֶץ וְכָל צְבָאָם. וַיְכַל אֱלֹהִים בַּיּוֹם הַשְּׁבִיעִי מְלַאכְתּוֹ אֲשֶׁר עָשָׂה, וַיִּשְׁבֹּת בַּיּוֹם הַשְּׁבִיעִי מִכָּל מְלַאכְתּוֹ אֲשֶׁר עָשָׂה. וַיְבָרֶךְ אֱלֹהִים אֶת יוֹם הַשְּׁבִיעִי וַיְקַדֵּשׁ אֹתוֹ, כִּי בוֹ שָׁבַת מִכָּל מְלַאכְתּוֹ אֲשֶׁר בָּרָא אֱלֹהִים לַעֲשׂוֹת.

בְּחוֹל מַתְחִילִין כָּאן
On a weeknight, begin here. Glance at the wine and say:

סַבְרִי מָרָנָן. בָּרוּךְ אַתָּה יְיָ, אֱלֹהֵינוּ מֶלֶךְ הָעוֹלָם, בּוֹרֵא פְּרִי הַגָּפֶן.

(On Friday night, add the orange text.)

בָּרוּךְ אַתָּה יְיָ, אֱלֹהֵינוּ מֶלֶךְ הָעוֹלָם, אֲשֶׁר בָּחַר בָּנוּ מִכָּל עָם, וְרוֹמְמָנוּ מִכָּל לָשׁוֹן, וְקִדְּשָׁנוּ בְּמִצְוֹתָיו. וַתִּתֶּן לָנוּ יְיָ אֱלֹהֵינוּ בְּאַהֲבָה (שַׁבָּתוֹת לִמְנוּחָה וּ) מוֹעֲדִים לְשִׂמְחָה, חַגִּים וּזְמַנִּים לְשָׂשׂוֹן, אֶת יוֹם (הַשַּׁבָּת הַזֶּה וְאֶת יוֹם) חַג הַמַּצּוֹת הַזֶּה, וְאֶת יוֹם טוֹב מִקְרָא קֹדֶשׁ הַזֶּה, זְמַן חֵרוּתֵנוּ, (בְּאַהֲבָה) מִקְרָא קֹדֶשׁ, זֵכֶר לִיצִיאַת מִצְרָיִם. כִּי בָנוּ בָחַרְתָּ וְאוֹתָנוּ קִדַּשְׁתָּ מִכָּל הָעַמִּים, (וְשַׁבָּת) וּמוֹעֲדֵי קָדְשֶׁךָ (בְּאַהֲבָה וּבְרָצוֹן) בְּשִׂמְחָה וּבְשָׂשׂוֹן הִנְחַלְתָּנוּ. בָּרוּךְ אַתָּה יְיָ, מְקַדֵּשׁ (הַשַּׁבָּת וְ) יִשְׂרָאֵל וְהַזְּמַנִּים.

On Motza'ei Shabbos, continue on the following page.

(One who has said שֶׁהֶחֱיָנוּ during candle lighting should not say it here.)

בָּרוּךְ אַתָּה יְיָ, אֱלֹהֵינוּ מֶלֶךְ הָעוֹלָם, שֶׁהֶחֱיָנוּ וְקִיְּמָנוּ וְהִגִּיעָנוּ לִזְמַן הַזֶּה.

שׁוֹתֶה הַכּוֹס בִּישִׁיבָה בַּהֲסִבַּת שְׂמֹאל דֶּרֶךְ חֵרוּת:
Drink the entire cup without pause while seated, reclining on the left side as a sign of freedom. (One who cannot drink the entire cup should drink at least most of it.)

Prepare the meal of Hashem, the exalted King. This is the meal of Hashem and His Shechinah.

יוֹם It was **the sixth day** of the creation of the world. **The heaven and the earth and all of their** many **creations were completed. By the seventh day, Hashem finished His work** of creating the world, **which He had done, and He rested on the seventh day from all His work, which He had done. Hashem blessed the seventh day and made it holy, because on that** day He rested **from all His work** - the world **that Hashem created** to continuously function.

Attention, gentlemen. Blessed are You, Hashem, our God, King of the world, Who creates the fruit of the vine.

בָּרוּךְ Blessed are You, Hashem, our God, King of the world, Who chose us at Har Sinai **from all** the other **nations.** He raised us above **all** those nations—each one with its **language**— and made us holy by giving us **His mitzvos. You, Hashem, our God, gave us, with love,** (days of Shabbos for rest and) festivals for happiness, Yamim Tovim and times for rejoicing, including **this day** of (Shabbos and this day of) **the Yom Tov of Pesach and this Yom Tov of holy gathering,** when we come together to daven to Hashem and praise Him, **the time of our freedom.** You gave us this day with love. **This is a day of a holy gathering,** when we come together to daven to Hashem and praise Him; **a reminder of Yetzias Mitzrayim. For You chose us and You made us holy** and distinguished **from** among **all** the other **nations** of the world, **and You have given us,** (with love and good will,) **with joy and happiness, Your holy** (Shabbos) **and Yamim Tovim as an** everlasting **heritage. Blessed are You, Hashem, Who makes** (the day of Shabbos,) B'nei **Yisrael and the times** of Yamim Tovim **holy.**

בָּרוּךְ Blessed are You, Hashem, our God, King of the world, Who has given us life, kept us alive, and enabled us to reach this special time.

MINHAGIM

Although having someone else fill one's cup is a sign of freedom, the minhag of the Rebbeim was to fill their cups on their own.

A DEEPER LOOK

Q Drinking four cups is a mitzvah Derabanan. Why do we not say a brachah on this mitzvah?

A We do not say a brachah on a mitzvah that is not completed at one time. Because we interrupt between the four cups, (with Maggid, Shulchan Orech, etc.) we do not say a brachah on the mitzvah of drinking them.

בְּמוֹצָאֵי שַׁבָּת מְקַדְּשִׁים יַקְנְהַ"ז. יַיִן, קִדּוּשׁ, נֵר, הַבְדָּלָה, זְמַן:

On Motza'ei Shabbos, continue with the following:

Glance at the Yom Tov candles while saying the following brachah:

בָּרוּךְ אַתָּה יְיָ, אֱלֹהֵינוּ מֶלֶךְ הָעוֹלָם, בּוֹרֵא מְאוֹרֵי הָאֵשׁ.

בָּרוּךְ אַתָּה יְיָ, אֱלֹהֵינוּ מֶלֶךְ הָעוֹלָם, הַמַּבְדִּיל בֵּין קֹדֶשׁ לְחֹל, בֵּין אוֹר לְחֹשֶׁךְ, בֵּין יִשְׂרָאֵל לָעַמִּים, בֵּין יוֹם הַשְּׁבִיעִי לְשֵׁשֶׁת יְמֵי הַמַּעֲשֶׂה. בֵּין קְדֻשַּׁת שַׁבָּת לִקְדֻשַּׁת יוֹם טוֹב הִבְדַּלְתָּ, וְאֶת יוֹם הַשְּׁבִיעִי מִשֵּׁשֶׁת יְמֵי הַמַּעֲשֶׂה קִדַּשְׁתָּ. הִבְדַּלְתָּ וְקִדַּשְׁתָּ אֶת עַמְּךָ יִשְׂרָאֵל בִּקְדֻשָּׁתֶךָ. בָּרוּךְ אַתָּה יְיָ, הַמַּבְדִּיל בֵּין קֹדֶשׁ לְקֹדֶשׁ.

(One who has said שֶׁהֶחֱיָנוּ during candle lighting should not say it here.)

בָּרוּךְ אַתָּה יְיָ, אֱלֹהֵינוּ מֶלֶךְ הָעוֹלָם, שֶׁהֶחֱיָנוּ וְקִיְּמָנוּ וְהִגִּיעָנוּ לִזְמַן הַזֶּה.

שׁוֹתֶה הַכּוֹס בִּישִׁיבָה בַּהֲסִבַּת שְׂמֹאל דֶּרֶךְ חֵרוּת:
Drink the entire cup without pause while seated, reclining on the left side as a sign of freedom. (One who cannot drink the entire cup should drink at least most of it.)

בָּרוּךְ Blessed are You, Hashem, our God, King of the world, Who creates the multi-colored lights of fire.

בָּרוּךְ Blessed are You, Hashem, our God, King of the world, Who separates between what is holy and what is ordinary, between light and darkness, between B'nei Yisrael and the other nations, and between the seventh day—Shabbos—and the six work days of the week. You have separated between the holiness of Shabbos and the holiness of Yom Tov, and You have made the seventh day holy above the six work days of the week. You have set apart and made holy Your nation, B'nei Yisrael, with Your holiness. Blessed are You, Hashem, Who separates between the holiness of Shabbos and the holiness of Yom Tov.

בָּרוּךְ Blessed are You, Hashem, our God, King of the world, Who has given us life, kept us alive, and enabled us to reach this special time.

STORY

The Rebbeim had in their possession the Alter Rebbe's Kiddush cup. The cup had the dried remains of the last Kiddush that the Alter Rebbe made while in the town of Pyene. (The Alter Rebbe passed away that Motza'ei Shabbos.)

This holy cup was placed on the table during the Rebbeim's Seder until somehow the cup was lost.

MINHAGIM

When the Seder takes place on Motza'ei Shabbos and Havdalah is made in Kiddush, the "Minhag Beis Harav" (minhag of the Rebbeim) is not to bring the candles closer or join the wicks together for the brachah of "borei m'orei ha'esh." Also, they would not look at the fingernails by the light of the flame, as is done on a regular Motza'ei Shabbos. Instead, they would just look at the candles while saying the brachah.

DID YOU KNOW?

Q Why do we lean to the left?

A We lean to the left and not to any other direction because:

- Leaning on your back or stomach is considered "lying," not "leaning;"

- We do not lean to the right because:

  a. Most people use their right hand to eat, so leaning on the right side is impractical.

  b. Our windpipe is located on the left side of our throat, and the food pipe is on the right. Leaning to the right would mean that the food first passes the windpipe on its way to the food-pipe. This might cause the food to enter the windpipe, resulting in choking.

וְנוֹטֵל יָדָיו וְאֵינוֹ מְבָרֵךְ:

All present now wash their hands in the following manner:

- Pick up the cup containing the water in your right hand. Pass it to your left hand and pour three times on your right hand. Then pass the cup to your right hand and pour three times on your left hand. (It is customary to hold the cup with a towel when pouring.)

- A little water from the final pouring should remain in the left hand, which is then rubbed over both hands together.

- Dry your hands.

- The brachah al netilas yadayim is not said.

 A DEEPER LOOK

Q Why is the brachah of עַל נְטִילַת יָדַיִם not said after washing for urchatz?

A There is a minority opinion that it is not necessary to wash one's hands before eating wet food. Although the halachah does not follow that opinion, a brachah is not said because of the rule, סָפֵק בְּרָכוֹת לְהָקֵל - when there is a doubt (in this case, different opinions) concerning a brachah, it is not said.

 DID YOU KNOW?

Q Why do we wash our hands before karpas?

A Before touching wet food to eat it a person should wash his hands. Even someone who doesn't normally do this during the year should do so on Pesach, in order to arouse the children's curiosity and lead them to ask questions.

נוֹטֵל פָּחוֹת מִכַּזַּיִת כַּרְפַּס וְטוֹבֵל בְּמֵי מֶלַח אוֹ חֹמֶץ וִיבָרֵךְ:

Take less than a kezayis of the karpas, dip it into
salt water, and say the following brachah.

Bear in mind that this brachah also applies to the
bitter herbs of Marror and Korech.

בָּרוּךְ אַתָּה יְיָ, אֱלֹהֵינוּ מֶלֶךְ הָעוֹלָם, בּוֹרֵא פְּרִי הָאֲדָמָה.

Blessed are You, Hashem, our God, King of the world,
Who creates the fruit of the earth.

יְכַוֵּן לְהוֹצִיא גַּם הַמָּרוֹר בִּבְרָכָה זוֹ:

Eat the karpas without leaning.

A DEEPER LOOK

Q Why do we eat less than a kezayis of karpas?

A If one were to eat a kezayis of karpas, there would be a machlokes whether he should say a brachah achronah (borei nefashos) or not. Since the purpose of eating karpas—to arouse curiosity—can be achieved by eating less than a kezayis, we specifically eat less than a kezayis for then a brachah achronah is not said according to all opinions.

MINHAGIM

Q Do we lean when we eat the karpas?

A The instructions in the Alter Rebbe's Haggadah do not indicate either way. However, our minhag is not to lean.

Also, most opinions rule that leaning is not required for karpas.

MINHAGIM

After eating karpas, any remaining pieces are not returned to the kaarah, and from this point on there are only five items on the kaarah.

DID YOU KNOW?

The letters of the word כַּרְפַּס can be rearranged to read ס' פרך, which hints to the **sixty** myriad (600,000) men who performed **back-breaking** work in Mitzrayim.

וְיִקַּח מַצָּה הָאֶמְצָעִית וּפוֹרְסָהּ לִשְׁנַיִם חֵלֶק אֶחָד גָּדוֹל מֵחֲבֵרוֹ וְחֵלֶק הַגָּדוֹל יַנִּיחַ לְאֲפִיקוֹמָן וְהַקָּטָן מַנִּיחַ בֵּין הַב׳ מַצּוֹת.

While still covered by the cloth, break the middle matzah into two pieces, one larger than the other.

Break the larger piece into five pieces, then wrap it in cloth and set aside to serve as Afikoman.

The smaller piece remains between the two whole matzos.

A DEEPER LOOK

Q Why don't we break the top matzah?

A There is a rule: אֵין מַעֲבִירִין עַל הַמִּצְוָה — if there is something available to be used for a mitzvah (such as any of the matzos in the kaarah), we should not pass it by and use something else instead.

The brachah of Hamotzi, said later in the Seder, must be said over a whole matzah. When reaching to hold the matzah for the brachah, our hands will encounter the top one first. Therefore, it should be used for the brachah, and must remain whole.

DID YOU KNOW?

Q Why is it the larger piece that gets saved for Afikoman?

A The Afikoman is a very important part of the Seder because it is eaten in place of the Korban Pesach. Therefore we put the larger piece away for it.

WORD POWER

Q What does the word "Afikoman" mean?

A In Aramaic it means to "bring out food" to the table.

In Greek, Afikoman means something which is eaten after the meal (dessert).

MINHAGIM

Q Why do some people "steal" the Afikoman?

A The minhag to "steal" the Afikoman is said to be based on the Gemara which says that we "grab matzah" on the night of Pesach in order to keep the children awake.

However, the Rebbeim did not have such a minhag because it could introduce children to the idea of stealing.

STORY

The Rebbe Rashab would break the Afikoman piece into five smaller pieces. Once, it broke into six pieces and he put one piece on the side.

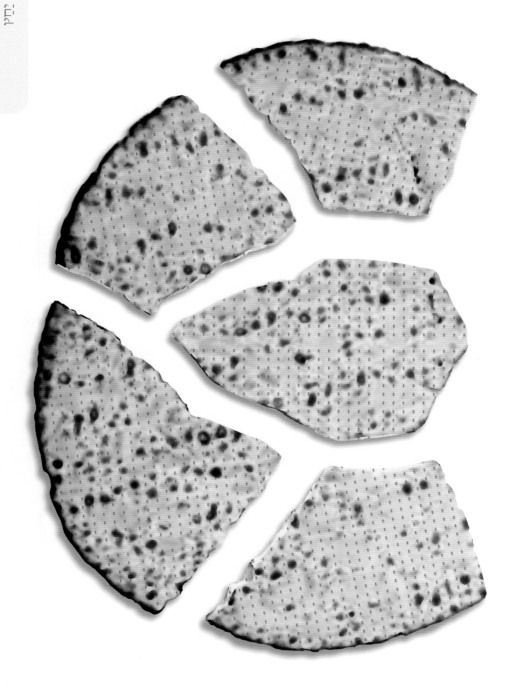

Q Why is it customary to wrap the Afikoman in cloth?

A When B'nei Yisrael fled from Mitzrayim, they wrapped the matzah and marror leftover from the Korban Pesach meal in their clothing. To commemorate this, we wrap the Afikoman in a cloth.

Q Why do we break a matzah into pieces before starting maggid?

A The mitzvah is to say the Haggadah in front of "lechem oni"—poor man's bread, which is represented by the broken matzah.

 וּמַגְבִּיהַ הַקְּעָרָה שֶׁיֵּשׁ בָּהּ הַמַּצּוֹת וְיֹאמַר:

Uncover the matzos partially and say:

הָא לַחְמָא עַנְיָא

דִּי אֲכָלוּ אַבְהָתָנָא בְּאַרְעָא דְמִצְרָיִם.

כֹּל דִּכְפִין יֵיתֵי וְיֵכוֹל,

כֹּל דִּצְרִיךְ יֵיתֵי וְיִפְסַח.

הַשַּׁתָּא הָכָא,

לְשָׁנָה הַבָּאָה בְּאַרְעָא דְיִשְׂרָאֵל.

הַשַּׁתָּא עַבְדִין,

לְשָׁנָה הַבָּאָה בְּנֵי חוֹרִין.

Cover the matzos.

הָא This is the bread of suffering
that our ancestors ate in the land of Egypt.

Let **all those who are hungry come and eat** with us.
Let **all those who are in need come** join us
for the **Pesach** Seder.

This year we are **here** in galus;
next year we will be **in Eretz Yisrael.**

This year we are **slaves**;
next year we will be **free people.**

NUSACH

Q How can we refer to the matzah in front of us as "the bread of suffering that our ancestors ate," when it is not the same matzah?

A We find a similar thing in the passuk where Hashem says that some *mann* should be kept in a jar "so that they see the bread that I fed them in the desert," even though the actual *mann* that they "were **fed**" was already eaten, and no longer existed.

We mean to say that this is the same **kind** of *mann* and matzah as they had then; not the same actual piece.

MINHAGIM

Even though it says in the Haggadah to lift the kaarah at this point, at the Rebbeim's Seder table they would only uncover the matzos slightly, and not lift the kaarah.

HISTORY

Q Why are the words לְשָׁנָה הַבָּאָה בְּנֵי חוֹרִין in Hebrew, while the rest of the paragraph is in Aramaic?

A This paragraph was written while the Jews were in galus in Bavel, and Aramaic was the language that everyone spoke at the time.

The Chachamim wrote the last words in Hebrew so that the Babylonians ruling them wouldn't understand what was being said. If they did, they would have thought that the Jews were planning to rebel against them.

NUSACH

Our nusach is to say הָא with a tzeirei under the ה, and the word is written this way numerous times in Tanach.

This nusach is also found in the siddur of the Arizal, who explains why it should be pronounced this way according to Kabbalah.

מְסַלְּקִין הַקְּעָרָה עִם הַמַּצּוֹת לְצַד אַחֵר וּמוֹזְגִין כּוֹס ב' וְכָאן הַבֵּן שׁוֹאֵל מַה נִּשְׁתַּנָּה:

Move the kaarah with the matzah to a side.

Pour the second cup.

Here the child asks, "Mah Nishtanah…"
Afterwards, all others say it in an undertone.

Minhag Chabad is to say it as written on the following page.

מַה נִּשְׁתַּנָּה הַלַּיְלָה הַזֶּה מִכָּל הַלֵּילוֹת.

1. שֶׁבְּכָל הַלֵּילוֹת אֵין אָנוּ מַטְבִּילִין אֲפִילוּ פַּעַם אֶחָת הַלַּיְלָה הַזֶּה שְׁתֵּי פְעָמִים.

2. שֶׁבְּכָל הַלֵּילוֹת אָנוּ אוֹכְלִין חָמֵץ אוֹ מַצָּה, הַלַּיְלָה הַזֶּה כֻּלּוֹ מַצָּה.

3. שֶׁבְּכָל הַלֵּילוֹת אָנוּ אוֹכְלִין שְׁאָר יְרָקוֹת, הַלַּיְלָה הַזֶּה מָרוֹר.

4. שֶׁבְּכָל הַלֵּילוֹת אָנוּ אוֹכְלִין בֵּין יוֹשְׁבִין וּבֵין מְסֻבִּין, הַלַּיְלָה הַזֶּה כֻּלָּנוּ מְסֻבִּין.

DID YOU KNOW?

Q Why is the Mah Nishtanah asked by a child?

A The Navi Hoshe'a quotes Hashem speaking about the time that He took us out of Mitzrayim, and said: כִּי נַעַר יִשְׂרָאֵל וָאֹהֲבֵהוּ - "Yisrael was a child and I loved him." By having a child ask the four questions, we awaken Hashem's fatherly love towards us.

מַה **What** makes **this night different from all the** other **nights** of the year?

1. **On all** other **nights we do not** need to **dip** our food **even once.** Why **on this night** do we dip **twice**—karpas into salt water, and marror into charoses?

2. **On all** other **nights we** may **eat** either **chametz or matzah.** Why **on this night** do we eat **only matzah?**

3. **On all** other **nights we eat any kind of vegetables.** Why **on this night** do we eat **marror?**

4. **On all** other **nights we eat** either **sitting** upright **or leaning.** Why **on this night** do **we all** eat **leaning?**

 **A DEEPER LOOK**

Q Why do we move away the Seder plate at this point?

A In order to make the children curious and cause them to ask, "We haven't eaten yet, so why are they taking away the food?" This will cause them to ask other questions, which is an important part of the Seder.

 SEDER ᴼᶠ ᴛʜᴇ SEDER

Q Why do we pour the second cup of wine at this point if we don't have to hold it until much later in Maggid?

A To make the children curious and cause them to ask more questions.

Minhag Chabad is to say it as written below:

טאַטע, אִיךְ װעל בַּא דִיר פְרֶעגְן פִיר קַשְׁיוֹת.

מַה נִּשְׁתַּנָּה הַלַּיְלָה הַזֶּה מִכָּל הַלֵּילוֹת.

וואָס אִיז אַנְדֶערְשׁ דִי נאַכְט פוּן פֶּסַח פוּן אַלֶע נֶעכְט פוּן אַ גאַנְץ יאָר.

דִי עֶרְשְׁטֶע קַשְׁיָא אִיז:

1 **שֶׁבְּכָל הַלֵּילוֹת אֵין אָנוּ מַטְבִּילִין אֲפִילוּ פַּעַם אֶחָת הַלַּיְלָה הַזֶּה שְׁתֵּי פְעָמִים.**

אַלֶע נֶעכְט פוּן אַ גאַנְץ יאָר טוּנְקֶען מִיר נִיט אַיין אֲפִילוּ אַיין מאָל, אָבֶּער דִי נאַכְט פוּן פֶּסַח טוּנְקֶען מִיר אַיין צְווֵיי מאָל: אַיין מאָל כַּרְפַּס אִין זאַלְץ וואַסֶער, אוּן דֶעם צְווֵייטן מאָל מָרוֹר אִין חֲרֹסֶת.

דִי צְווֵייטֶע קַשְׁיָא אִיז:

2 **שֶׁבְּכָל הַלֵּילוֹת אָנוּ אוֹכְלִין חָמֵץ אוֹ מַצָּה, הַלַּיְלָה הַזֶּה כֻּלּוֹ מַצָּה.**

אַלֶע נֶעכְט פוּן אַ גאַנְץ יאָר עֶסָן מִיר חָמֵץ אָדֶער מַצָּה, אָבֶּער דִי נאַכְט פוּן פֶּסַח עֶסָן מִיר נאָר מַצָּה.

דִי דְרִיטֶע קַשְׁיָא אִיז:

3 **שֶׁבְּכָל הַלֵּילוֹת אָנוּ אוֹכְלִין שְׁאָר יְרָקוֹת, הַלַּיְלָה הַזֶּה מָרוֹר.**

אַלֶע נֶעכְט פוּן אַ גאַנְץ יאָר עֶסָן מִיר אַלֶע עֶרְלֵיי גְרִינְסְן, אָבֶּער דִי נאַכְט פוּן פֶּסַח עֶסָן מִיר בִּיטֶערֶע גְרִינְסְן.

דִי פֶערְטֶע קַשְׁיָא אִיז:

4 **שֶׁבְּכָל הַלֵּילוֹת אָנוּ אוֹכְלִין בֵּין יוֹשְׁבִין וּבֵין מְסֻבִּין, הַלַּיְלָה הַזֶּה כֻּלָּנוּ מְסֻבִּין.**

אַלֶע נֶעכְט פוּן אַ גאַנְץ יאָר עֶסָן מִיר סַיי זִיצֶענְדִיקֶערְהֵייט אוּן סַיי אָנְגֶעלֶענְטֶערְהֵייט, אָבֶּער דִי נאַכְט פוּן פֶּסַח עֶסָן מִיר אַלֶע אָנְגֶעלֶענְטֶערְהֵייט.

(טאַטע, אִיךְ האָב בַּא דִיר גֶעפְרֶעגְט פִיר קַשְׁיוֹת, יֶעצְט גִיב בִּיטֶע מִיר אַ תֵּירוּץ.)

MINHAGIM

It is our custom to say *Tatte ich vell bei dir fregen fir kashyes*—Father, I will ask you four questions—before we say Mah Nishtanah.

Everyone does this, even if their father is not present at the Seder.

SEDER OF THE SEDER

Q What is the reason for the order of the four questions?

A We ask the questions in the order of how these things appear during the Seder.

- Dipping occurs first, so we ask about dipping first.

- Next is yachatz, breaking the matzah, so the next question is about matzah and chametz.

- Then we eat marror, so the third question is about marror.

- Even though we lean at the very beginning of the Seder when we drink the Kiddush wine, we ask this question last. This is because in ancient times, people would regularly lean while they ate, so there was nothing unusual about it. When people stopped doing this, and leaning on Pesach became unique, this question was added on to the end of Mah Nishtanah.

NUSACH

There are different customs regarding the order of the four questions. The order in our nusach is found in many early sources, including:

- The Mishnah in Yerushalmi
- Rif
- Rosh
- R' Amram Gaon
- R' Saadia Gaon
- Rambam
- Tur
- Avudraham
- Abarbanel
- Arizal

The questions also follow this order in the first printed Haggadah (in 1485).

HISTORY

In the times of the Beis Hamikdash, when the Korban Pesach was eaten on this night, another question was asked:

"On all other nights we eat roasted, boiled, or cooked meat. Why on this night do we eat only roasted meat?"

NUSACH

Q The fact that we drink four cups of wine is pretty unusual. Why don't we ask about that in the Mah Nishtanah?

A The mitzvah to drink four cups is not Min Hatorah, whereas all of the four questions ask about things that are connected to a mitzvah Min Hatorah:

1. The dipping is performed with the marror, which is a mitzvah Min Hatorah,

2. Eating matzah is Min Hatorah,

3. Eating marror is Min Hatorah,

4. We lean while eating matzah, which is Min Hatorah.

WORD POWER

Q Throughout the Seder, we dip three times: karpas into saltwater, marror into charoses, and the marror of korech into charoses. So why do we talk about dipping *twice*?

A We count the dipping of marror and korech as only one dipping. This is because they are just two ways of performing the same mitzvah. (See also "A Deeper Look" on page 97.)

וּמַחֲזִירִין הַקְּעָרָה וּמְגַלִּין מִקְצָת הַפַּת וְאוֹמְרִים עֲבָדִים וְכוּ':

Bring back the kaarah, uncover the matzos partially, and say:

עֲבָדִים הָיִינוּ לְפַרְעֹה בְּמִצְרָיִם, וַיּוֹצִיאֵנוּ יְיָ אֱלֹהֵינוּ מִשָּׁם בְּיָד חֲזָקָה וּבִזְרֹעַ נְטוּיָה, וְאִלּוּ לֹא הוֹצִיא הַקָּדוֹשׁ בָּרוּךְ הוּא אֶת אֲבוֹתֵינוּ מִמִּצְרַיִם, הֲרֵי אָנוּ וּבָנֵינוּ וּבְנֵי בָנֵינוּ מְשֻׁעְבָּדִים הָיִינוּ לְפַרְעֹה בְּמִצְרָיִם. וַאֲפִילוּ כֻּלָּנוּ חֲכָמִים כֻּלָּנוּ נְבוֹנִים כֻּלָּנוּ יוֹדְעִים אֶת הַתּוֹרָה, מִצְוָה עָלֵינוּ לְסַפֵּר בִּיצִיאַת מִצְרַיִם, וְכָל הַמַּרְבֶּה לְסַפֵּר בִּיצִיאַת מִצְרַיִם הֲרֵי זֶה מְשֻׁבָּח.

STORY

When the Frierdiker Rebbe was a child, his father asked him why we don't say a brachah on the mitzvah of Sippur Yetzias Mitzrayim on Pesach night. The Frierdiker Rebbe did not know the answer.

His father, the Rebbe Rashab, told him that when he was a child, he was asked the same question by his father, the Rebbe Maharash, and did not know the answer.

In turn, the Rebbe Maharash told him that when he was a child, he was asked the same question by his father, the Tzemach Tzedek, and did not know the answer.

The Tzemach Tzedek told him that when he was a child, he was asked the same question by his grandfather, the Alter Rebbe, and did not know the answer.

The Mitteler Rebbe was present, and answered that we already said a brachah on it when we said "זֵכֶר לִיצִיאַת מִצְרַיִם" in Kiddush.

The Alter Rebbe answered that the entire Maggid is actually one large brachah, as can be seen at its conclusion where we say the brachah "אֲשֶׁר גְּאָלָנוּ." We do not say a brachah for saying another brachah! (For this reason, also, we do not make a brachah before saying birkas hamazon.)

See "Nusach" for additional answers.

NUSACH

Q If it is a mitzvah to tell the story of Yetzias Mitzrayim, why don't we say a brachah on it?

A There are many answers to this, including:

1. We already mentioned Yetzias Mitzrayim at the end of Krias Shema in Maariv, and made a brachah before and after it.

2. We do not say a brachah on a mitzvah that is not completed all at once. Because we interrupt the story, we do not say a brachah before telling it.

See "Story" for additional answers.

HISTORY

Q How can the Haggadah say that if Hashem hadn't taken us out of Mitzrayim, we would still be Paraoh's slaves? Wouldn't he eventually have died?

A All Egyptian rulers were called Paraoh, not just the one who lived at the time of Yetzias Mitzrayim. Although by the time the Haggadah was written, Egypt had lost its power and there were no more Paraohs, if we had in fact not been taken out by Hashem, Egypt would have continued being powerful, because of the Jews living there.

עֲבָדִים **We were slaves to Paraoh in Egypt, and Hashem, our God, took us out from there with a strong hand and an outstretched arm.**

If Hashem had not taken our fathers out of Egypt, then the Egyptian empire would have remained powerful and **we, our children and our children's children, would** still **be enslaved to a Paraoh in Egypt.**

Therefore, **even if we are all wise, we are all understanding,** and **we all know the Torah, we** still **have the mitzvah to tell the story of Yetzias Mitzrayim. Everyone who discusses Yetzias Mitzrayim at length is praiseworthy.**

DID YOU KNOW?

Q Isn't the mitzvah to remember Yetzias Mitzrayim every day of the year, not just on Pesach?

A There are many differences between the mitzvah we have during the year and the mitzvah we have on Pesach, including:

1. During the year, it's enough to remember Yetzias Mitzrayim in our minds. On Pesach, we must actually talk about it.

2. During the year, Yetzias Mitzrayim can be briefly mentioned. On Pesach, we must discuss it in length, and tell it as a story.

A DEEPER LOOK

Q Are women also obligated to talk about the story of Yetzias Mitzrayim, even though it is a מִצְוַת עֲשֵׂה שֶׁהַזְמַן גְּרָמָה - a mitzvah that comes at a certain time, which they normally do not need to keep?

A Yes. According to Tosfos they are obligated Min Hatorah, and according to other opinions they are only obligated Miderabanan. The Alter Rebbe holds like the second opinion, that they are obligated Miderabanan.

מַעֲשֶׂה בְּרַבִּי אֱלִיעֶזֶר וְרַבִּי יְהוֹשֻׁעַ וְרַבִּי אֶלְעָזָר בֶּן עֲזַרְיָה וְרַבִּי עֲקִיבָא וְרַבִּי טַרְפוֹן, שֶׁהָיוּ מְסֻבִּין בִּבְנֵי בְרַק, וְהָיוּ מְסַפְּרִים בִּיצִיאַת מִצְרַיִם כָּל אוֹתוֹ הַלַּיְלָה, עַד שֶׁבָּאוּ תַלְמִידֵיהֶם וְאָמְרוּ לָהֶם: רַבּוֹתֵינוּ, הִגִּיעַ זְמַן קְרִיאַת שְׁמַע שֶׁל שַׁחֲרִית.

אָמַר רַבִּי אֶלְעָזָר בֶּן עֲזַרְיָה: הֲרֵי אֲנִי כְּבֶן שִׁבְעִים שָׁנָה, וְלֹא זָכִיתִי שֶׁתֵּאָמֵר יְצִיאַת מִצְרַיִם בַּלֵּילוֹת, עַד שֶׁדְּרָשָׁהּ בֶּן זוֹמָא, שֶׁנֶּאֱמַר:

לְמַעַן תִּזְכֹּר אֶת יוֹם צֵאתְךָ מֵאֶרֶץ מִצְרַיִם כֹּל יְמֵי חַיֶּיךָ.

"יְמֵי חַיֶּיךָ" הַיָּמִים, "כֹּל יְמֵי חַיֶּיךָ" לְהָבִיא הַלֵּילוֹת.

וַחֲכָמִים אוֹמְרִים: "יְמֵי חַיֶּיךָ" הָעוֹלָם הַזֶּה, "כֹּל יְמֵי חַיֶּיךָ" לְהָבִיא לִימוֹת הַמָּשִׁיחַ.

מַעֲשֶׂה Everyone should discuss Yetzias Mitzrayim at length, even someone whose ancestors were not slaves in Egypt, such as a Kohen, Levi or a ger. We see this from the **story of Rabbi Eliezer** (a Levi), **Rabbi Yehoshua** (a Levi), **Rabbi Elazar ben Azaryah** (a Kohen), **Rabbi Akiva** (a descendant of gerim) **and Rabbi Tarfon** (a Kohen) **who were gathered** at a Seder **in B'nei Brak,** and were discussing Yetzias Mitzrayim at length, **all that night, until,** in the morning, **their students came and told them: "Our masters! The time has come** to say the **morning Krias Shema!"**

אָמַר **Rabbi Elazar ben Azaryah said** to them, **"I am like a man of seventy years old,** because I am weak from learning day and night. Nevertheless, **I did not succeed** in proving that in addition to the obligation to mention Yetzias Mitzrayim during the day, there is also an obligation **to mention Yetzias Mitzrayim during the night, until Ben Zoma explained it** as follows: "The Torah **says:** 'Eat the matzah and the Korban Pesach **so that you will remember the day you left Egypt throughout all the days of your life.'**

"The words **'the days of your life'** teach us that we must mention Yetzias Mitzrayim during **the daytime.** The extra word '*all* **(the days of your life)'** is written **to include** all times of the day — **the nights** as well as the days."

The Chachamim, however, **explain** the passuk differently: "The words 'the days of your life' teach us that we must mention Yetzias Mitzrayim **these days,** during galus. The extra word '*all* (the days of your life)' teaches us that we will be mentioning Yetzias Mitzrayim even after **the coming of Moshiach.**"

A DEEPER LOOK

Q Why are the Tanna'im listed in this specific order?

A They are listed in the order they were sitting. The most important was R' Elazar ben Azaryah, as he was the Nassi; he therefore sat in the middle. R' Eliezer and R' Yehoshua, both of whom were R' Akiva's teachers, were the next in importance; they therefore sat to the right of the Nassi. On the other side of the Nassi sat the remaining Tanna'im, R' Akiva and R' Tarfon.

HISTORY

Q Why did Rabbi Elazar ben Azaryah say that he is *like* a seventy year old man?

A He was actually in his teens, but on the day he was appointed Nassi, his physical appearance aged a lot, and he looked like an old man.

Also, because he learned Torah day and night, his body became weak like an old man.

בָּרוּךְ הַמָּקוֹם, בָּרוּךְ הוּא, בָּרוּךְ שֶׁנָּתַן תּוֹרָה לְעַמּוֹ יִשְׂרָאֵל, בָּרוּךְ הוּא, כְּנֶגֶד אַרְבָּעָה בָנִים דִּבְּרָה תוֹרָה: אֶחָד חָכָם, וְאֶחָד רָשָׁע, וְאֶחָד תָּם, וְאֶחָד שֶׁאֵינוֹ יוֹדֵעַ לִשְׁאוֹל.

חָכָם מַה הוּא אוֹמֵר:

מָה הָעֵדֹת וְהַחֻקִּים וְהַמִּשְׁפָּטִים אֲשֶׁר צִוָּה יְיָ אֱלֹהֵינוּ אֶתְכֶם. וְאַף אַתָּה אֱמָר לוֹ כְּהִלְכוֹת הַפֶּסַח, אֵין מַפְטִירִין אַחַר הַפֶּסַח אֲפִיקוֹמָן.

רָשָׁע מַה הוּא אוֹמֵר:

מָה הָעֲבֹדָה הַזֹּאת לָכֶם. "לָכֶם" וְלֹא לוֹ, וּלְפִי שֶׁהוֹצִיא אֶת עַצְמוֹ מִן הַכְּלָל, כָּפַר בְּעִקָּר. וְאַף אַתָּה הַקְהֵה אֶת שִׁנָּיו וֶאֱמָר לוֹ: בַּעֲבוּר זֶה עָשָׂה יְיָ לִי בְּצֵאתִי מִמִּצְרָיִם, "לִי" וְלֹא לוֹ, אִלּוּ הָיָה שָׁם לֹא הָיָה נִגְאָל.

WORD POWER

Q Why do we refer to Hashem as הַמָּקוֹם - "The Place?"

A Since Hashem is "larger" than the universe, Hashem is like the "place" in which the universe exists.

SEDER OF THE SEDER

Q Why are the four sons listed in this particular order?

A They are listed in order of their intelligence:

The chacham comes first.

The rasha is mentioned second, because he, too, is smart, but uses his abilities for bad things.

The tam is mentioned before the she'aino yode'a lish'ol because he at least knows how to ask something.

A DEEPER LOOK

Q The chacham seemingly also excludes himself from the nation by asking "What are these mitzvos which Hashem commanded *you*?" If so, how is he different than the rasha?

A When the chacham says "you," he does not mean that he is not part of it. Rather he is addressing his question to those who actually experienced Yetzias Mitzrayim.

To show that he does not exclude himself, he says "ה' אֱלֹהֵינוּ - Hashem **our** God."

בָּרוּךְ Blessed is Hashem, Who is called "The Place" because He is in every place, blessed be He. Blessed is Hashem, Who gave the Torah to His nation, B'nei Yisrael, blessed be He. The Torah speaks of four sons: One is wise, one is wicked, one is simple and one does not know how to ask.

חָכָם What does the wise one say?

"What are the eidos (mitzvos which are to commemorate something that happened), the chukim (mitzvos which have no reason that we can understand), and the mishpatim (logical mitzvos) which Hashem, our God, has commanded you?" When responding to his question, in addition to telling him the story of Yetzias Mitzrayim, you should also teach him the rest of hilchos Pesach, up to the last halachah: One is not allowed to eat any dessert after eating of the Korban Pesach so its taste will remain in his mouth.

רָשָׁע What does the wicked one say?

"What is this avodah of yours?" He says "of yours," and does not include himself. By excluding himself from the community and not considering himself involved with this mitzvah, he shows that he denies his obligation to fulfill Hashem's mitzvos, the most important part of living as a Jew.

When responding to his question, in addition to telling him the story of Yetzias Mitzrayim, you should also "blunt his teeth," (meaning, speak harshly to him) and say to him as follows: The Torah says that a father should tell his son, "Hashem did miracles for me when I left Egypt, in order that I keep His mitzvos, such as these mitzvos of Korban Pesach, eating matzah, and eating marror."

The Torah says "for me," meaning the father, but does not include the wicked son. If the wicked son would have been there, he would not have been redeemed.

תָּם מַה הוּא אוֹמֵר:

מַה זֹאת, וְאָמַרְתָּ אֵלָיו: בְּחֹזֶק יָד הוֹצִיאָנוּ יְיָ מִמִּצְרַיִם מִבֵּית עֲבָדִים.

וְשֶׁאֵינוֹ יוֹדֵעַ לִשְׁאוֹל,

אַתְּ פְּתַח לוֹ, שֶׁנֶּאֱמַר: וְהִגַּדְתָּ לְבִנְךָ בַּיּוֹם הַהוּא לֵאמֹר: בַּעֲבוּר זֶה עָשָׂה יְיָ לִי בְּצֵאתִי מִמִּצְרָיִם.

יָכוֹל מֵרֹאשׁ חֹדֶשׁ, תַּלְמוּד לוֹמַר: "בַּיּוֹם הַהוּא." אִי בַּיּוֹם הַהוּא, יָכוֹל מִבְּעוֹד יוֹם, תַּלְמוּד לוֹמַר: "בַּעֲבוּר זֶה," בַּעֲבוּר זֶה לֹא אָמַרְתִּי אֶלָּא בְּשָׁעָה שֶׁיֵּשׁ מַצָּה וּמָרוֹר מֻנָּחִים לְפָנֶיךָ.

תָּם What does the simple one say?

"**What is this** celebration about?" When responding to his question, **you should say to him:** We are celebrating the fact that **Hashem took us out from Egypt, from the house of slaves, with a strong hand.**

וְשֶׁאֵינוֹ As for the son who does not know how to ask.

You must open up the conversation **for him, as it says** in the Torah: **You should tell your son on that** first **day** of Pesach. **Say to him:** "**Hashem performed** miracles **for me when I left Egypt, in order that** I keep His mitzvos, such as **these** mitzvos of Korban Pesach, eating matzah, and marror."

יָכוֹל One might think that the discussion of Yetzias Mitzrayim must begin from Rosh Chodesh Nissan, because that was when Moshe Rabbeinu gave B'nei Yisrael instructions concerning Yetzias Mitzrayim. Therefore, the Torah **says,** "You should tell your son about Yetzias Mitzrayim **on that day**" (the day of the Korban Pesach), in order **to teach** us that we begin when we bring the Korban Pesach.

If the Torah would only say "**on that day,**" however, **one might think** that he should begin **while it is still daytime** on Erev Pesach, because the previous passuk speaks about the Korban Pesach, which was brought in the afternoon of Erev Pesach. **To teach** us otherwise, the Torah **says** that the father should tell his son, "It is **because of these** mitzvos—Korban Pesach, eating matzah and marror—that Hashem did miracles for me when I left Egypt." **You can only say "because of these** mitzvos" on the night of Pesach itself **when you have** the obligation to eat **matzah and marror.**

WORD POWER

חָכָם מַה הוּא — אוֹמֵר, רָשָׁע מַה הוּא — אוֹמֵר

These words can be translated to mean:
"**A chacham** reveals **what he is** by what and how he **speaks.**
A rasha reveals **what he is** by what and how he **speaks.**"

DID YOU KNOW?

There are two opinions regarding whether one still needs to say the Haggadah if he has no matzah or marror.

1. According to many Rishonim, one does not need to say the Haggadah.

2. According to other opinions, however, the expression, "בְּשָׁעָה שֶׁיֵּשׁ מַצָּה וּמָרוֹר מֻנָּחִים לְפָנֶיךָ — when there is matzah and marror in front of you," means at the **time** when it is a **mitzvah** to have them. Therefore, if they are not actually available, one still must say the Haggadah.

מִתְּחִלָּה עוֹבְדֵי עֲבוֹדָה זָרָה הָיוּ אֲבוֹתֵינוּ, וְעַכְשָׁו קֵרְבָנוּ הַמָּקוֹם לַעֲבֹדָתוֹ, שֶׁנֶּאֱמַר: וַיֹּאמֶר יְהוֹשֻׁעַ אֶל כָּל הָעָם, כֹּה אָמַר יְיָ אֱלֹהֵי יִשְׂרָאֵל. בְּעֵבֶר הַנָּהָר יָשְׁבוּ אֲבוֹתֵיכֶם מֵעוֹלָם, תֶּרַח אֲבִי אַבְרָהָם וַאֲבִי נָחוֹר, וַיַּעַבְדוּ אֱלֹהִים אֲחֵרִים.

וָאֶקַּח אֶת אֲבִיכֶם אֶת אַבְרָהָם מֵעֵבֶר הַנָּהָר, וָאוֹלֵךְ אוֹתוֹ בְּכָל אֶרֶץ כְּנָעַן, וָאַרְבֶּה אֶת זַרְעוֹ וָאֶתֶּן לוֹ אֶת יִצְחָק. וָאֶתֵּן לְיִצְחָק אֶת יַעֲקֹב וְאֶת עֵשָׂו, וָאֶתֵּן לְעֵשָׂו אֶת הַר שֵׂעִיר לָרֶשֶׁת אוֹתוֹ, וְיַעֲקֹב וּבָנָיו יָרְדוּ מִצְרָיִם.

בָּרוּךְ שׁוֹמֵר הַבְטָחָתוֹ לְיִשְׂרָאֵל, בָּרוּךְ הוּא, שֶׁהַקָּדוֹשׁ בָּרוּךְ הוּא חִשַּׁב אֶת הַקֵּץ לַעֲשׂוֹת כְּמָה שֶׁאָמַר לְאַבְרָהָם אָבִינוּ בִּבְרִית בֵּין הַבְּתָרִים, שֶׁנֶּאֱמַר: וַיֹּאמֶר לְאַבְרָם: יָדֹעַ תֵּדַע כִּי גֵר יִהְיֶה זַרְעֲךָ בְּאֶרֶץ לֹא לָהֶם, וַעֲבָדוּם וְעִנּוּ אֹתָם, אַרְבַּע מֵאוֹת שָׁנָה. וְגַם אֶת הַגּוֹי אֲשֶׁר יַעֲבֹדוּ דָּן אָנֹכִי, וְאַחֲרֵי כֵן יֵצְאוּ בִּרְכֻשׁ גָּדוֹל.

HISTORY

Q Which of our ancestors are we referring to when we say that they served idols?

A We are referring to Terach (Avraham's father) and the people before him, who did indeed serve idols.

DID YOU KNOW?

Q What was this promise that Hashem made to our ancestors?

A Hashem promised Avraham Avinu to eventually take B'nei Yisrael out of Egypt. After this, Hashem promised the Nevi'im throughout history that He would destroy those who rise up against B'nei Yisrael.

A DEEPER LOOK

Q If Hashem promised Avraham that He would redeem us from Egypt, why throughout the Torah does He continually remind us that He indeed redeemed us, as if it was something which He did not *have* to do?

A Hashem had only promised to physically take us out of Egypt. But in the end Hashem also rescued us from the forty-nine levels of tumah to which we had sunk during Galus Mitzrayim.

מִתְּחִלָּה **Originally,** before Avraham Avinu, **our ancestors served idols. But now, Hashem brought us close to His avodah, as it says** in Sefer Yehoshua: **Yehoshua said to the entire nation, "This is what Hashem, the God of** B'nei **Yisrael, said, 'Your ancestors—Terach, the father of Avraham Avinu and the father of Nachor—used to live on the other side of the** Pras river, **and they served other gods.**

וָאֶקַּח **But I took your father Avraham from across the river, and I led him throughout the whole land of Canaan. I increased his descendants and gave him his son Yitzchak, and to Yitzchak I gave** two sons, **Yaakov and Esav. I gave Har Sei'ir as an inheritance to Esav** for him to live there, so as not be counted as part of Yitzchak's descendants, about whom I promised to Avraham that they would be slaves in a strange land, and would later be redeemed and brought back to Eretz Yisrael. Whereas **Yaakov and his sons** did **go down to Egypt,** and are therefore considered Yitzchak's descendants, the ones whom I will 'bring back' to Eretz Yisrael."

בָּרוּךְ **Blessed is** Hashem **Who keeps His promise** regarding B'nei **Yisrael** throughout the generations. **Blessed be He, because Hashem calculated the end** of Galus Mitzrayim, in order **to** keep the promise and **do as He had said to Avraham Avinu at the Bris Bein Hab'sarim. As it says** in the Torah: Hashem **said to Avram, "You should know that your descendants will be strangers in a land that is not theirs, where** their masters **will force them to be slaves and make them suffer for four hundred years. I will also judge** and punish **the nation whom they will serve, and afterwards they will leave with great wealth."**

צָרִיךְ לְהַגְבִּיהַּ הַכּוֹס וּלְכַסּוֹת הַפַּת כֵּן כָּתַב הָאֲרִ"י זַ"ל:

Cover the matzos.
The Arizal wrote that one should raise the cup (as is done during Kiddush) while saying the following paragraph.

וְהִיא שֶׁעָמְדָה

לַאֲבוֹתֵינוּ וְלָנוּ,

שֶׁלֹּא אֶחָד בִּלְבַד עָמַד עָלֵינוּ לְכַלּוֹתֵנוּ

אֶלָּא שֶׁבְּכָל דּוֹר וָדוֹר עוֹמְדִים עָלֵינוּ לְכַלּוֹתֵנוּ,

וְהַקָּדוֹשׁ בָּרוּךְ הוּא מַצִּילֵנוּ מִיָּדָם.

יַעֲמִיד הַכּוֹס וִיגַלֶּה הַפַּת:

Place the cup on the table and uncover the matzos.

 SEDER OF THE SEDER

Q Why do we cover the matzos before saying וְהִיא שֶׁעָמְדָה?

A The Haggadah should be said over the matzah. However, this paragraph is said while holding the cup of wine. To avoid "embarrassing" the matzah, we cover it so it should not "see" our focus on the wine.

 A DEEPER LOOK

כֵּן כָּתַב הָאֲרִ"י זַ"ל

Q Why does the Alter Rebbe quote the source of the instruction here, unlike the rest of the instructions?

A According to halachah, one does not have to hold the cup for this paragraph because it is not a "song of praise." Therefore, the Alter Rebbe quotes the instruction from the Arizal to show that it is only according to Kabbalah that one should hold the cup at this point.

וְהִיא **This**—Hashem's promise throughout the generations—**is what has stood by** and protected **our fathers and us.**

We needed the protection of this promise throughout all the generations **because not just** Paraoh **alone rose up against us to** utterly **destroy us,**

but in every generation there are **those** who **rise up against us to** utterly **destroy us,**

and Hashem saves us from their hands.

צֵא וּלְמַד מַה בִּקֵּשׁ לָבָן הָאֲרַמִּי לַעֲשׂוֹת לְיַעֲקֹב אָבִינוּ, שֶׁפַּרְעֹה לֹא גָזַר אֶלָּא עַל הַזְּכָרִים, וְלָבָן בִּקֵּשׁ לַעֲקוֹר אֶת הַכֹּל, שֶׁנֶּאֱמַר: אֲרַמִּי אֹבֵד אָבִי, וַיֵּרֶד מִצְרַיְמָה וַיָּגָר שָׁם בִּמְתֵי מְעָט, וַיְהִי שָׁם לְגוֹי גָּדוֹל עָצוּם וָרָב.

"וַיֵּרֶד מִצְרַיְמָה," אָנוּס עַל פִּי הַדִּבּוּר.

"וַיָּגָר שָׁם," מְלַמֵּד שֶׁלֹּא יָרַד יַעֲקֹב אָבִינוּ לְהִשְׁתַּקֵּעַ בְּמִצְרַיִם אֶלָּא לָגוּר שָׁם, שֶׁנֶּאֱמַר: וַיֹּאמְרוּ אֶל פַּרְעֹה לָגוּר בָּאָרֶץ בָּאנוּ, כִּי אֵין מִרְעֶה לַצֹּאן אֲשֶׁר לַעֲבָדֶיךָ, כִּי כָבֵד הָרָעָב בְּאֶרֶץ כְּנָעַן, וְעַתָּה יֵשְׁבוּ נָא עֲבָדֶיךָ בְּאֶרֶץ גֹּשֶׁן.

צֵא **Leave** the story of Yetzias Mitzrayim **and learn** how Hashem saves us in every generation, for example, how Hashem saved us from **what Lavan Ha'arami wanted to do to Yaakov Avinu.**

Paraoh only decreed to drown **the male** babies in the Nile River**, but Lavan wanted to ruin** Yaakov's **entire** family**, as it says** in the Torah: **Lavan Ha'arami wanted to destroy my forefather** Yaakov Avinu and his family after they ran away from him. Yaakov then **went down to Egypt and stayed-over there** with his family, who were **few in number, and he became a nation there—great, mighty and numerous.**

"He went down to Egypt." – The only reason Yaakov went down to Egypt was because he was **forced by** Hashem's **decree** to Avraham that his descendants will be strangers in a foreign land.

"And stayed-over there." – These words **teach** us that Yaakov Avinu did **not go down to Egypt to settle, but only to live there temporarily. As it says** in the Torah: The shevatim **said to Paraoh, "We have come to stay-over in the land** until the hunger passes, **because there is no pasture for your servants' sheep in the land of Canaan since the famine is severe** there. **Now, please, let your servants dwell in the land of Goshen."**

 **WORD POWER**

Q In what way was Yaakov Avinu "forced" to go down to Egypt?

A Yaakov went down willingly. As the passuk says, "וַיֵּרֶד - and he went down," and does not say הוּרַד - "he was brought down." However, because Hashem had promised Avraham Avinu that his descendants "would be strangers" in a foreign land, Hashem arranged a famine—causing Yaakov to decide willingly to go down to Egypt—to ensure that the decree would be fulfilled. In this sense, the circumstances "forced" him to go down to Egypt.

"בְּמְתֵי מְעָט," כְּמָה שֶׁנֶּאֱמַר: בְּשִׁבְעִים נֶפֶשׁ יָרְדוּ אֲבֹתֶיךָ
מִצְרַיְמָה, וְעַתָּה שָׂמְךָ יְיָ אֱלֹהֶיךָ כְּכוֹכְבֵי הַשָּׁמַיִם לָרֹב.

"וַיְהִי שָׁם לְגוֹי," מְלַמֵּד שֶׁהָיוּ יִשְׂרָאֵל מְצֻיָּנִים שָׁם.

"גָּדוֹל עָצוּם," כְּמָה שֶׁנֶּאֱמַר: וּבְנֵי יִשְׂרָאֵל פָּרוּ וַיִּשְׁרְצוּ וַיִּרְבּוּ
וַיַּעַצְמוּ בִּמְאֹד מְאֹד וַתִּמָּלֵא הָאָרֶץ אֹתָם.

"וָרָב," כְּמָה שֶׁנֶּאֱמַר: וָאֶעֱבֹר עָלַיִךְ וָאֶרְאֵךְ מִתְבּוֹסֶסֶת בְּדָמָיִךְ,
וָאֹמַר לָךְ בְּדָמַיִךְ חֲיִי, וָאֹמַר לָךְ בְּדָמַיִךְ חֲיִי. רְבָבָה כְּצֶמַח הַשָּׂדֶה
נְתַתִּיךְ וַתִּרְבִּי וַתִּגְדְּלִי וַתָּבֹאִי בַּעֲדִי עֲדָיִים, שָׁדַיִם נָכֹנוּ וּשְׂעָרֵךְ
צִמֵּחַ, וְאַתְּ עֵרֹם וְעֶרְיָה.

"Few in number" **As it says** in the Torah: When **your fathers went down to Egypt,** they were **seventy people, and now, Hashem, your God, has made you as many as the stars of the heavens.**

"And he became a nation there" – **This teaches** us **that** B'nei **Yisrael stood out** in Egypt as a different nation because they did not change their names, language, religion, or style of clothing.

"Great, mighty" As it says in the Torah: **B'nei Yisrael were fruitful** because their babies did not die; **they increased greatly** because they had six children from one pregnancy; **they multiplied and became very, very mighty, and the land became filled with them.'**

"And numerous" As the Navi Yechezkel **said** in the name of Hashem: **I passed over you and saw you lying in your blood, and I said to you, "As much as** they torture you and make **you bleed** that's how much **you will live** and multiply," **and I said to you, "As much as** they torture you and make you **bleed** that's how much **you will live** and multiply." And indeed, **I caused you to flourish** and multiply **like the plants of the field, and you increased and grew and became very beautiful; your body matured, your hair grew long,** and you became a strong nation. The time came to redeem you, **but you were naked and bare** of any mitzvos.

HISTORY

Q In what way were B'nei Yisrael "noticeable" while they were in Egypt?

A They did not change their names, their language, their religion, or the way they dressed. In all these areas, they kept their distinct identity and were noticeably Jewish. They did not try to become more "Egyptian."

וַיָּרֵעוּ אֹתָנוּ הַמִּצְרִים וַיְעַנּוּנוּ, וַיִּתְּנוּ עָלֵינוּ עֲבֹדָה קָשָׁה.

"וַיָּרֵעוּ אֹתָנוּ הַמִּצְרִים," כְּמָה שֶׁנֶּאֱמַר: הָבָה נִתְחַכְּמָה לוֹ, פֶּן יִרְבֶּה, וְהָיָה כִּי תִקְרֶאנָה מִלְחָמָה, וְנוֹסַף גַּם הוּא עַל שֹׂנְאֵינוּ, וְנִלְחַם בָּנוּ וְעָלָה מִן הָאָרֶץ.

"וַיְעַנּוּנוּ," כְּמָה שֶׁנֶּאֱמַר: וַיָּשִׂימוּ עָלָיו שָׂרֵי מִסִּים לְמַעַן עַנֹּתוֹ בְּסִבְלֹתָם, וַיִּבֶן עָרֵי מִסְכְּנוֹת לְפַרְעֹה, אֶת פִּתֹם וְאֶת רַעַמְסֵס.

"וַיִּתְּנוּ עָלֵינוּ עֲבֹדָה קָשָׁה," כְּמָה שֶׁנֶּאֱמַר: וַיַּעֲבִדוּ מִצְרַיִם אֶת בְּנֵי יִשְׂרָאֵל בְּפָרֶךְ. וַיְמָרְרוּ אֶת חַיֵּיהֶם בַּעֲבֹדָה קָשָׁה בְּחֹמֶר וּבִלְבֵנִים וּבְכָל עֲבֹדָה בַּשָּׂדֶה, אֵת כָּל עֲבֹדָתָם אֲשֶׁר עָבְדוּ בָהֶם בְּפָרֶךְ.

The Torah continues in the following passuk:

The Egyptians treated us badly, they made us suffer, and they made us do hard work.

"The Egyptians treated us badly" – Not only did they make them suffer but they made a point of *looking* for ways to harm B'nei Yisrael. **As it says** in the Torah: Paraoh said to the Egyptians, **"Come, let us deal with** B'nei Yisrael **in a sly way** so that **they will not multiply. Because if a war were to break out, they would join our enemies, fight against us** and conquer us, **and** then **leave the land."**

"They made us suffer" – **As it says** in the Torah: **The** Egyptians **appointed supervisors** over B'nei Yisrael **to make them suffer** by making them do **the** hard **work** the Egyptians needed, **and they built storage houses for Paraoh,** called **Pisom and Ra'amses.**

"And they made us do hard work" – **As it says** in the Torah: **The Egyptians made B'nei Yisrael do backbreaking work. They made their lives bitter with hard work** – by making them work **with mortar and bricks and all kinds of work in the fields. All** the **work that** the Egyptians **made them do was crushingly hard.**

 **WORD POWER**

Q What's the difference between וַיָּרֵעוּ — "they treated us badly," and, וַיְעַנּוּנוּ — "they made us suffer?"

A In addition to appointing slave masters to "make us suffer," the Egyptians were always **seeking** ways to "treat us badly." This can be seen from the passuk brought to show that "they treated us badly," which discusses the Egyptians scheming and planning.

וַנִּצְעַק אֶל יְיָ אֱלֹהֵי אֲבוֹתֵינוּ, וַיִּשְׁמַע יְיָ אֶת קֹלֵנוּ, וַיַּרְא אֶת עָנְיֵנוּ וְאֶת עֲמָלֵנוּ וְאֶת לַחֲצֵנוּ.

"וַנִּצְעַק אֶל יְיָ אֱלֹהֵי אֲבוֹתֵינוּ," כְּמָה שֶׁנֶּאֱמַר: וַיְהִי בַיָּמִים הָרַבִּים הָהֵם וַיָּמָת מֶלֶךְ מִצְרַיִם, וַיֵּאָנְחוּ בְנֵי יִשְׂרָאֵל מִן הָעֲבֹדָה וַיִּזְעָקוּ, וַתַּעַל שַׁוְעָתָם אֶל הָאֱלֹהִים מִן הָעֲבֹדָה.

"וַיִּשְׁמַע יְיָ אֶת קֹלֵנוּ," כְּמָה שֶׁנֶּאֱמַר: וַיִּשְׁמַע אֱלֹהִים אֶת נַאֲקָתָם, וַיִּזְכֹּר אֱלֹהִים אֶת בְּרִיתוֹ אֶת אַבְרָהָם אֶת יִצְחָק וְאֶת יַעֲקֹב.

"וַיַּרְא אֶת עָנְיֵנוּ," זוֹ פְּרִישׁוּת דֶּרֶךְ אֶרֶץ, כְּמָה שֶׁנֶּאֱמַר: וַיַּרְא אֱלֹהִים אֶת בְּנֵי יִשְׂרָאֵל, וַיֵּדַע אֱלֹהִים.

"וְאֶת עֲמָלֵנוּ," אֵלּוּ הַבָּנִים, כְּמָה שֶׁנֶּאֱמַר: כָּל הַבֵּן הַיִּלּוֹד הַיְאֹרָה תַּשְׁלִיכֻהוּ, וְכָל הַבַּת תְּחַיּוּן.

"וְאֶת לַחֲצֵנוּ," זֶה הַדְּחַק, כְּמָה שֶׁנֶּאֱמַר: וְגַם רָאִיתִי אֶת הַלַּחַץ אֲשֶׁר מִצְרַיִם לֹחֲצִים אֹתָם.

WORD POWER

The word לַחֲצֵנוּ can mean our physical hardship and oppression, but here it means our stress and pressure. Not only did the Egyptians make us work hard, they also pressured us to work so much that we had no peace or rest.

A DEEPER LOOK

One may think that the passuk "Hashem saw B'nei Yisrael and Hashem took note" proves that the passuk "He saw our suffering" refers to the fact that Jewish husbands and wives were split up. This is not the case, as it does not prove that at all.

Rather, with the proof-passuk "Hashem saw B'nei Yisrael" the Haggadah intends merely to prove that Hashem indeed "saw our suffering." The fact that Jewish husbands and wives split up is a side point, explaining the word עָנְיֵנוּ. Therefore, the words זו פְּרִישׁוּת דֶּרֶךְ אֶרֶץ should be read as if in parentheses.

The Torah continues in the following passuk:

We cried out to Hashem, the God of our fathers, and Hashem heard our voice and saw our suffering, our labor, and our pressure.

"We cried out to Hashem, the God of our fathers" – **As it says** in the Torah: **During the long period** that Moshe lived in Midyan, **the king of Egypt died. B'nei Yisrael groaned from the hard work, and they cried out. Their cries, caused by the hard work, went up to Hashem.**

"And Hashem heard our voice" – **As it says** in the Torah: **Hashem heard** B'nei Yisrael's **groaning, and Hashem remembered the promise He made to Avraham, Yitzchak, and Yaakov** that he would bring B'nei Yisrael to Eretz Yisrael.

"And saw our suffering" – "Our suffering" **refers to** Paraoh's decree to **separate the** Jewish husbands and wives so they wouldn't be able to have **normal** family life. Hashem saw B'nei Yisrael's suffering, **as it says** in the Torah: **Hashem saw B'nei Yisrael, and Hashem took** their cries **to heart.**

"Our hard work" – **This refers to the children** who are referred to in Torah as a man's strength. Paraoh issued a decree against the children. **As it says** in the Torah: Paraoh said, **"Throw every newborn boy into the** Nile **river, and keep every girl alive."**

"And our pressure" – **This refers to the pressure** that the Egyptians applied to B'nei Yisrael, allowing them no rest. Hashem saw the pressure, **as it says** in the Torah: Hashem said, **"I have also seen the pressure with which the Egyptians are pressuring them."**

וַיּוֹצִיאֵנוּ יְיָ מִמִּצְרַיִם בְּיָד חֲזָקָה וּבִזְרֹעַ נְטוּיָה וּבְמֹרָא גָּדוֹל וּבְאֹתוֹת וּבְמֹפְתִים.

"וַיּוֹצִיאֵנוּ יְיָ מִמִּצְרַיִם," לֹא עַל יְדֵי מַלְאָךְ וְלֹא עַל יְדֵי שָׂרָף וְלֹא עַל יְדֵי שָׁלִיחַ, אֶלָּא הַקָּדוֹשׁ בָּרוּךְ הוּא בִּכְבוֹדוֹ וּבְעַצְמוֹ, שֶׁנֶּאֱמַר: וְעָבַרְתִּי בְאֶרֶץ מִצְרַיִם בַּלַּיְלָה הַזֶּה, וְהִכֵּיתִי כָל בְּכוֹר בְּאֶרֶץ מִצְרַיִם מֵאָדָם וְעַד בְּהֵמָה, וּבְכָל אֱלֹהֵי מִצְרַיִם אֶעֱשֶׂה שְׁפָטִים, אֲנִי יְיָ. "וְעָבַרְתִּי בְאֶרֶץ מִצְרַיִם," אֲנִי וְלֹא מַלְאָךְ. "וְהִכֵּיתִי כָל בְּכוֹר בְּאֶרֶץ מִצְרַיִם," אֲנִי וְלֹא שָׂרָף. "וּבְכָל אֱלֹהֵי מִצְרַיִם אֶעֱשֶׂה שְׁפָטִים," אֲנִי וְלֹא הַשָּׁלִיחַ. "אֲנִי יְיָ," אֲנִי הוּא וְלֹא אַחֵר.

"בְּיָד חֲזָקָה," זֶה הַדֶּבֶר, כְּמָה שֶׁנֶּאֱמַר: הִנֵּה יַד יְיָ הוֹיָה בְּמִקְנְךָ אֲשֶׁר בַּשָּׂדֶה, בַּסּוּסִים בַּחֲמֹרִים בַּגְּמַלִּים בַּבָּקָר וּבַצֹּאן, דֶּבֶר כָּבֵד מְאֹד.

"וּבִזְרֹעַ נְטוּיָה," זוֹ הַחֶרֶב, כְּמָה שֶׁנֶּאֱמַר: וְחַרְבּוֹ שְׁלוּפָה בְּיָדוֹ נְטוּיָה עַל יְרוּשָׁלָיִם.

The Torah continues in the following passuk:

Hashem took us out of Egypt with a strong hand, with an outstretched arm, with a great display, with signs and with wonders.

"Hashem took us out of Egypt" – We were taken out of Egypt, **not through a malach, not through** a fiery malach called **a Saraf, and not through a messenger. Rather, it was Hashem Himself in His glory** Who took us out, **as it says** in the Torah: **I will pass through the land of Egypt on the night** of Pesach, **and I will slay every firstborn in the land of Egypt, from man to animal, and I will carry out judgments and punish all the gods of Egypt. I, Hashem,** will do this personally.

"I will pass through the land of Egypt on this night" – **I and not a malach.** "And I will slay every firstborn in the land of Egypt." – **I and not a Saraf.** "And I will carry out judgments and punish all the gods of Egypt." – **I and not a messenger.** "I, Hashem." – **It is I and no one else.**

"With a strong hand" — **This refers to the** plague of **Dever, as it says** in the Torah when Moshe warned the Egyptians: **Behold, the hand of Hashem will** punish you **by placing a very deadly disease on your animals in the fields — on the horses, the donkeys, the camels, the cattle, and the flock.**

"With an outstretched arm" — **This refers to the** plague of Makkas Bechoros when Hashem killed their firstborn with a **sword. As it says** in Divrei Hayamim regarding this sword: **His sword drawn in His hand, stretched out over Yerushalayim.**

A DEEPER LOOK

Q Why did Hashem Himself have to save B'nei Yisrael from Egypt, and did not do it through a messenger?

A Because Egypt was so immoral and impure, Hashem did not want to send a holy angel there to punish them. Hashem, however, was able to punish them without actually going there, because He is able to cause things to happen merely by commanding them to be.

"וּבְמֹרָא גָּדוֹל," זֶה גִּלּוּי שְׁכִינָה, כְּמָה שֶׁנֶּאֱמַר: אוֹ הֲנִסָּה אֱלֹהִים לָבוֹא לָקַחַת לוֹ גוֹי מִקֶּרֶב גּוֹי בְּמַסֹּת בְּאֹתֹת וּבְמוֹפְתִים וּבְמִלְחָמָה וּבְיָד חֲזָקָה וּבִזְרוֹעַ נְטוּיָה וּבְמוֹרָאִים גְּדֹלִים, כְּכֹל אֲשֶׁר עָשָׂה לָכֶם יְיָ אֱלֹהֵיכֶם בְּמִצְרַיִם לְעֵינֶיךָ.

"וּבְאֹתוֹת," זֶה הַמַּטֶּה, כְּמָה שֶׁנֶּאֱמַר: וְאֶת הַמַּטֶּה הַזֶּה תִּקַּח בְּיָדֶךָ אֲשֶׁר תַּעֲשֶׂה בּוֹ אֶת הָאֹתֹת.

"וּבְמוֹפְתִים," זֶה הַדָּם, כְּמָה שֶׁנֶּאֱמַר: וְנָתַתִּי מוֹפְתִים בַּשָּׁמַיִם וּבָאָרֶץ—

בַּאֲמִירַת דָּם וָאֵשׁ וְתִימְרוֹת עָשָׁן יִשְׁפֹּךְ ג' שְׁפִיכוֹת וְאֵין לִטּוֹל בְּאֶצְבַּע לִשְׁפּוֹךְ כִּי אִם בְּכוֹס עַצְמוֹ וְיִשְׁפֹּךְ לְתוֹךְ כְּלִי שָׁבוּר (וִיכַוֵּן שֶׁהַכּוֹס הוּא סוֹד הַמַּלְכוּת וְשׁוֹפֵךְ מֵהַיַּיִן שֶׁבְּתוֹכוֹ סוֹד הָאַף וְהַזַּעַם שֶׁבָּא עַל יְדֵי כֹּחַ הַבִּינָה לְתוֹךְ כְּלִי שָׁבוּר סוֹד הַקְּלִפָּה שֶׁנִּקְרֵאת אָרוּר:)

- When saying the words, "דָם וְתִימְרוֹת עָשָׁן," spill a little bit of the wine in your cup three times—once during each phrase, preferably into a broken dish. (It is not Minhag Chabad to remove wine by dipping in a finger.)

- Have in mind that the cup symbolizes the sefirah of malchus (kingship),

which contains an element of "anger and fury." Using our power of binah (understanding), we pour out that element of "anger and fury" by spilling from the wine from the cup into a broken dish, which represents kelipah, i.e., that which is called "accursed." The remaining wine is called "wine that brings joy."

Spill while saying:

דָּם וָאֵשׁ וְתִימְרוֹת עָשָׁן.

דָּבָר אַחֵר:

2 Makkos	"בְּיָד חֲזָקָה" שְׁתַּיִם,
+ 2 Makkos	"וּבִזְרֹעַ נְטוּיָה" שְׁתַּיִם,
+ 2 Makkos	"וּבְמֹרָא גָּדוֹל" שְׁתַּיִם,
+ 2 Makkos	"וּבְאֹתוֹת" שְׁתַּיִם,
+ 2 Makkos	"וּבְמוֹפְתִים" שְׁתַּיִם.
= 10 Makkos	

"With a great display." — **This refers to the revelation of** Hashem's **Shechinah** during Makkas Bechoros and geulas Mitzrayim.

Hashem took us out of Egypt with a great display. **As it says** in the Torah: **Has any god performed miracles when coming to take for himself a nation from within another nation, by challenging** the enemy to test his greatness, **with signs and wonders, with war, with a strong hand, an outstretched arm, and with a great display, as all that Hashem, your God, did for you in Egypt before your eyes?**

"With signs." — **This** refers to the signs Hashem did with **the stick** of Moshe, turning it into a snake, and swallowing the other sticks. **As it says** in the Torah when Hashem commanded Moshe to go to Paraoh: **You shall take this stick in your hand, with which you will perform the signs.**

"And with wonders." — **This refers to the** plague of **Blood. As it says** in Sefer Yoel: **I will show wonders in heaven and on earth, of**

blood, fire, and pillars of smoke.

There is **another way** of deriving the plagues from this passuk: From the words **"with a strong hand"** we learn about **two** plagues – one from the word "hand" by itself, and one from the extra description "*strong* hand;" From the words **"with an outstretched arm"** we learn about **two** more plagues – one from the word "arm" by itself, and one from the extra description "*outstretched* arm;" From the words **"with great display"** we learn about **two** plagues – one from the word "display" by itself, and one from the extra description "*great* display;" from the plural expression of the word **"signs"** we learn about **two** more plagues; from the plural expression of the word **"wonders"** we learn about **two** more plagues.

 SEDER OF THE SEDER

 WORD POWER

Q Why are the plagues of Dever, Makkas Bechoros (referred to here as "cherev"), and Dam listed in the discussions here in the Haggadah, and why in this order, when they occurred in a different order?

A These three makkos demonstrate three levels of Hashem's punishments. He destroyed the Egyptians' **possessions** during the plague of Dever. Greater than that—He destroyed the Egyptian **people** during Makkas Bechoros.
Greater than that—He destroyed their **false gods,** by turning the Nile River—which the Egyptians served as a god—to blood, during the plague of Dam.

Q When the Haggadah says that the word וּבְמוֹפְתִים refers to "blood," is that the blood of Makkas Dam?

A Some mefarshim say that it refers to an incident that took place well before the ten makkos—when Hashem told Moshe that in order to get B'nei Yisrael to believe that he would lead them out of Mitzrayim, he should take water from the Nile, put it on dry land, and turn it into blood. However, it is more likely that it refers to Makkas Dam, as most mefarshim explain it.

אֵלּוּ עֶשֶׂר מַכּוֹת שֶׁהֵבִיא הַקָּדוֹשׁ בָּרוּךְ הוּא עַל הַמִּצְרִים בְּמִצְרַיִם, וְאֵלּוּ הֵן:

בַּאֲמִירַת עֶשֶׂר מַכּוֹת יִשְׁפֹּךְ עֲשֶׂר שְׁפִיכוֹת מֵהַכּוֹס עַצְמוֹ כַּנַּ"ל (וִיכַוֵּן בִּשְׁפִיכָה גַּם כֵּן כַּנַּ"ל) וּמַה שֶׁנִּשְׁאַר בַּכּוֹס (נַעֲשָׂה סוֹד יַיִן הַמְשַׂמֵּחַ לְכָךְ) לֹא יִשְׁפֹּךְ אֶלָּא יוֹסִיף יַיִן:

When listing the ten makkos, spill a little wine into the broken dish, once during each makkah, with the same kavanah as above.

דָּם, צְפַרְדֵּעַ, כִּנִּים, עָרוֹב, דֶּבֶר, שְׁחִין, בָּרָד, אַרְבֶּה, חֹשֶׁךְ, מַכַּת בְּכוֹרוֹת.

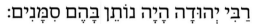

רַבִּי יְהוּדָה הָיָה נוֹתֵן בָּהֶם סִמָּנִים:

When saying the following three acronyms, spill a little wine into the broken dish, once for each acronym, with the same kavanah as above.

דְּצַ"ךְ, עֲדַ"שׁ, בְּאַחַ"ב.

DID YOU KNOW?

Q What was accomplished by Rabbi Yehudah's acronym of דְּצַ"ךְ עֲדַ"שׁ בְּאַחַ"ב?

A Sometimes we say אֵין מוּקְדָם וּמְאוּחָר בַּתּוֹרָה - things didn't necessarily happen in the order in which they appear in the Torah. In fact, in perek ק"ה of Tehillim, the ten makkos are mentioned in a different order. Rabbi Yehudah is telling us that the order of the makkos in the Torah is in fact the order in which they actually happened.

שְׁחִין

בָּרָד

אַרְבֶּה

חֹשֶׁךְ

מַכַּת בְּכוֹרוֹת

These are the ten plagues that Hashem brought upon the Egyptians in Egypt. They are:

Blood,
frogs,
lice,

wild beasts,
deadly disease in animals,
boils,

hail,
locusts,
darkness,
killing of the firstborn.

Rabbi Yehudah would refer to the ten plagues by their **roshei teivos** to help remember their order:

DeTZa"CH
ADa"SH
BeACHa"V.

WORD POWER

Q Does the grouping of the makkos to form the words דְּצַ"ךְ עֲדַ"שׁ בְּאַחַ"ב have any significance?

A There are many explanations regarding these words, including:

- Paraoh received a warning regarding the first two makkos represented in each word, and received no warning about the following makkah.

- The first three makkos (דְּצַ"ךְ) were performed by Aharon Hakohen. The next three makkos (עֲדַ"שׁ) were performed by Moshe Rabbeinu without using his special stick. The last four makkos (בְּאַחַ"ב) were performed by Moshe Rabbeinu with his special stick.

Refill your cup with wine.

רַבִּי יוֹסֵי הַגְּלִילִי אוֹמֵר: מִנַּיִן אַתָּה אוֹמֵר שֶׁלָּקוּ הַמִּצְרִים בְּמִצְרַיִם עֶשֶׂר מַכּוֹת וְעַל הַיָּם לָקוּ חֲמִשִּׁים מַכּוֹת, בְּמִצְרַיִם מַה הוּא אוֹמֵר: וַיֹּאמְרוּ הַחַרְטֻמִּם אֶל פַּרְעֹה אֶצְבַּע אֱלֹהִים הִיא. וְעַל הַיָּם מַה הוּא אוֹמֵר: וַיַּרְא יִשְׂרָאֵל אֶת הַיָּד הַגְּדֹלָה אֲשֶׁר עָשָׂה יְיָ בְּמִצְרַיִם, וַיִּירְאוּ הָעָם אֶת יְיָ, וַיַּאֲמִינוּ בַּיְיָ וּבְמשֶׁה עַבְדּוֹ. כַּמָּה לָקוּ בְאֶצְבַּע, עֶשֶׂר מַכּוֹת, אֱמוֹר מֵעַתָּה: בְּמִצְרַיִם לָקוּ עֶשֶׂר מַכּוֹת, וְעַל הַיָּם לָקוּ חֲמִשִּׁים מַכּוֹת.

See chart (next page) explaining the following three opinions.

רַבִּי Rabbi Yossi Haglili says: From where do you know to say that the Egyptians were struck by ten plagues in Egypt, and were struck by fifty plagues at the sea?

Concerning the plagues in Egypt, the Torah says: The sorcerers said to Paraoh, "It's the finger of Hashem." Concerning the plagues at the sea, the Torah says: B'nei Yisrael saw the great and mighty hand which Hashem used to fight and destroy the Egyptians, and the people feared Hashem. They believed in Hashem and in Moshe, His servant.

Now, how many plagues were the Egyptians struck with by "the finger of Hashem" in Egypt? Ten plagues. You must therefore say that if in Egypt, where the Egyptians were struck by a single finger, they were struck by ten plagues, at the sea, where they were struck by "Hashem's great hand" (which has five fingers), they must have been struck by five times that amount – fifty plagues.

רַבִּי אֱלִיעֶזֶר אוֹמֵר: מִנַּיִן שֶׁכָּל מַכָּה וּמַכָּה שֶׁהֵבִיא הַקָּדוֹשׁ בָּרוּךְ הוּא עַל הַמִּצְרִים בְּמִצְרַיִם הָיְתָה שֶׁל אַרְבַּע מַכּוֹת, שֶׁנֶּאֱמַר: יְשַׁלַּח בָּם חֲרוֹן אַפּוֹ, עֶבְרָה, וָזַעַם, וְצָרָה, מִשְׁלַחַת מַלְאֲכֵי רָעִים. "עֶבְרָה" אַחַת, "וָזַעַם" שְׁתַּיִם, "וְצָרָה" שָׁלֹשׁ, "מִשְׁלַחַת מַלְאֲכֵי רָעִים" אַרְבַּע, אֱמוֹר מֵעַתָּה: בְּמִצְרַיִם לָקוּ אַרְבָּעִים מַכּוֹת, וְעַל הַיָּם לָקוּ מָאתַיִם מַכּוֹת.

רַבִּי עֲקִיבָא אוֹמֵר: מִנַּיִן שֶׁכָּל מַכָּה וּמַכָּה שֶׁהֵבִיא הַקָּדוֹשׁ בָּרוּךְ הוּא עַל הַמִּצְרִים בְּמִצְרַיִם הָיְתָה שֶׁל חָמֵשׁ מַכּוֹת, שֶׁנֶּאֱמַר: יְשַׁלַּח בָּם חֲרוֹן אַפּוֹ, עֶבְרָה, וָזַעַם, וְצָרָה, מִשְׁלַחַת מַלְאֲכֵי רָעִים. "חֲרוֹן אַפּוֹ" אַחַת, "עֶבְרָה" שְׁתַּיִם, "וָזַעַם" שָׁלֹשׁ, "וְצָרָה" אַרְבַּע, "מִשְׁלַחַת מַלְאֲכֵי רָעִים" חָמֵשׁ, אֱמוֹר מֵעַתָּה: בְּמִצְרַיִם לָקוּ חֲמִשִּׁים מַכּוֹת, וְעַל הַיָּם לָקוּ חֲמִשִּׁים וּמָאתַיִם מַכּוֹת.

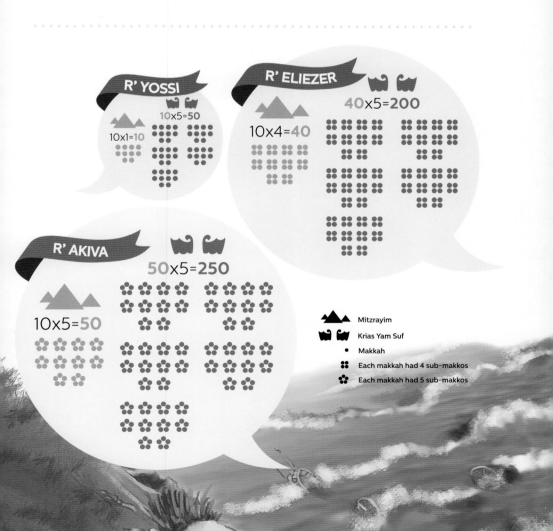

R' YOSSI
10x1=10
10x5=50

R' ELIEZER
40x5=200
10x4=40

R' AKIVA
50x5=250
10x5=50

Mitzrayim
Krias Yam Suf
Makkah
Each makkah had 4 sub-makkos
Each makkah had 5 sub-makkos

רַבִּי Rabbi Eliezer says: From where do we know that each individual plague that Hashem brought upon the Egyptians in Egypt and at the sea consisted of four sub-plagues?

We learn it from Tehillim where it says regarding the plagues:

Hashem sent forth against the Egyptians His fierce anger, fury, rage, misfortune, and a group of messengers of evil.

The word "fury" tells us about one sub-plague; the word "rage" makes two; "misfortune" makes three; and "a group of messengers of evil" makes four.

Now that you see from the passuk that each plague consisted of four sub-plagues, you must say that in Egypt, where the Egyptians were struck by a single finger, they were struck by ten plagues consisting of four each, totalling forty plagues, and at the sea, where they were struck five times that amount by "Hashem's great hand," they were struck by two hundred plagues.

רַבִּי Rabbi Akiva says: From where do we know that each individual plague that Hashem brought upon the Egyptians in Egypt and at the sea consisted of five sub-plagues?

We learn it from Tehillim where it says regarding the plagues:

Hashem sent forth against the Egyptians His fierce anger, fury, rage, misfortune, and a group of messengers of evil.

The words "His fierce anger" tells us about one sub-plague; the word "fury" makes two; the word "rage" makes three; "misfortune" makes four; and "a group of messengers of evil" makes five.

Now that you see from the passuk that each plague consisted of five sub-plagues, you must say that in Egypt, where the Egyptians were struck by a single finger, they were struck by ten plagues consisting of five each, totalling fifty plagues, and at the sea, where they were struck five times that amount by "Hashem's great hand," they were struck by two hundred and fifty plagues.

A DEEPER LOOK

Q How can these Tanna'im calculate that there were tens and hundreds of makkos, if everyone knows that there were *ten* makkos?

A There were ten **general** types of plagues, and each one had many details. For example, during Makkas Arov, wild animals killed people, and also tore up and destroyed the land as they walked on it.

כַּמָּה מַעֲלוֹת טוֹבוֹת לַמָּקוֹם עָלֵינוּ:

One should not interrupt the recital
of the fourteen stanzas of "Dayenu."

אִלּוּ הוֹצִיאָנוּ מִמִּצְרַיִם
וְלֹא עָשָׂה בָהֶם שְׁפָטִים — דַּיֵּנוּ.

אִלּוּ עָשָׂה בָהֶם שְׁפָטִים
וְלֹא עָשָׂה בֵאלֹהֵיהֶם — דַּיֵּנוּ.

אִלּוּ עָשָׂה בֵאלֹהֵיהֶם
וְלֹא הָרַג אֶת בְּכוֹרֵיהֶם — דַּיֵּנוּ.

אִלּוּ הָרַג אֶת בְּכוֹרֵיהֶם
וְלֹא נָתַן לָנוּ אֶת מָמוֹנָם — דַּיֵּנוּ.

אִלּוּ נָתַן לָנוּ אֶת מָמוֹנָם
וְלֹא קָרַע לָנוּ אֶת הַיָּם — דַּיֵּנוּ.

אִלּוּ קָרַע לָנוּ אֶת הַיָּם
וְלֹא הֶעֱבִירָנוּ בְתוֹכוֹ בֶּחָרָבָה — דַּיֵּנוּ.

אִלּוּ הֶעֱבִירָנוּ בְתוֹכוֹ בֶּחָרָבָה
וְלֹא שִׁקַּע צָרֵינוּ בְּתוֹכוֹ — דַּיֵּנוּ.

אִלּוּ שִׁקַּע צָרֵינוּ בְּתוֹכוֹ
וְלֹא סִפֵּק צָרְכֵּנוּ בַּמִּדְבָּר אַרְבָּעִים שָׁנָה — דַּיֵּנוּ.

WORD POWER

וְלֹא הֶעֱבִירָנוּ בְתוֹכוֹ בֶּחָרָבָה

The emphasis of this verse is on the last word, בֶּחָרָבָה - on completely dry land. We are not saying that "If Hashem had split the Yam Suf but not taken us through it—it would have been enough," because of what use would it have been if Hashem had split the Yam Suf, but did not take us through it?

Rather, we are saying that if Hashem would have taken us through the Yam Suf—but on a muddy path—it would have been enough. We are especially thankful that Hashem made it totally dry and comfortable for us to cross.

SEDER OF THE SEDER

Q **What wealth are we referring to when we say "If He had given us their *wealth*, but not split the Yam Suf?"**

A It does not mean the wealth that we took from what washed up **after** Krias Yam Suf, because then this sentence would be out of order.

Rather, it refers to the treasures the Egyptians hid, which B'nei Yisrael found during Makkas Choshech.

Hashem has showered **upon us so many good things!**

If Hashem **had taken us out of Egypt,**
but had not carried out judgments against the
Egyptians and punished **them**
— **it would have been** reason **enough for us** to thank Him.

If He had carried out judgments against the
Egyptians and punished **them,**
but had not destroyed their gods
— **it would have been** reason **enough for us** to thank Him.

If He had destroyed their gods,
but had not killed their firstborn
— **it would have been** reason **enough for us** to thank Him.

If He had killed their firstborn,
but had not given us their wealth
— **it would have been** reason **enough for us** to thank Him.

If He had given us their wealth during Makkas Choshech,
but had not hardened Paraoh's heart so that he gave chase,
leading Hashem to **split the sea for us**
— **it would have been** reason **enough for us** to thank Him.

If He had split the sea for us,
but had not taken us through it on completely **dry land**
— **it would have been** reason **enough for us** to thank Him.

If He had taken us through the sea on completely **dry land,**
but had not drowned our enemies in it
— **it would have been** reason **enough for us** to thank Him.

If He had drowned our enemies in the sea,
but had not supplied our needs in the
desert for forty years, and we would have
had to buy them from local
merchants
— **it would have been**
reason **enough for us** to
thank Him.

אִלּוּ סִפֵּק צָרְכֵּנוּ בַּמִּדְבָּר אַרְבָּעִים שָׁנָה
וְלֹא הֶאֱכִילָנוּ אֶת הַמָּן – דַּיֵּנוּ.

אִלּוּ הֶאֱכִילָנוּ אֶת הַמָּן
וְלֹא נָתַן לָנוּ אֶת הַשַּׁבָּת – דַּיֵּנוּ.

אִלּוּ נָתַן לָנוּ אֶת הַשַּׁבָּת
וְלֹא קֵרְבָנוּ לִפְנֵי הַר סִינַי – דַּיֵּנוּ.

אִלּוּ קֵרְבָנוּ לִפְנֵי הַר סִינַי
וְלֹא נָתַן לָנוּ אֶת הַתּוֹרָה – דַּיֵּנוּ.

אִלּוּ נָתַן לָנוּ אֶת הַתּוֹרָה
וְלֹא הִכְנִיסָנוּ לְאֶרֶץ יִשְׂרָאֵל – דַּיֵּנוּ.

אִלּוּ הִכְנִיסָנוּ לְאֶרֶץ יִשְׂרָאֵל
וְלֹא בָנָה לָנוּ אֶת בֵּית הַבְּחִירָה – דַּיֵּנוּ.

עַל אַחַת כַּמָּה וְכַמָּה טוֹבָה כְפוּלָה וּמְכֻפֶּלֶת לַמָּקוֹם עָלֵינוּ, שֶׁהוֹצִיאָנוּ מִמִּצְרַיִם, וְעָשָׂה בָהֶם שְׁפָטִים, וְעָשָׂה בֵאלֹהֵיהֶם, וְהָרַג אֶת בְּכוֹרֵיהֶם, וְנָתַן לָנוּ אֶת מָמוֹנָם, וְקָרַע לָנוּ אֶת הַיָּם, וְהֶעֱבִירָנוּ בְתוֹכוֹ בֶּחָרָבָה, וְשִׁקַּע צָרֵינוּ בְּתוֹכוֹ, וְסִפֵּק צָרְכֵּנוּ בַּמִּדְבָּר אַרְבָּעִים שָׁנָה, וְהֶאֱכִילָנוּ אֶת הַמָּן, וְנָתַן לָנוּ אֶת הַשַּׁבָּת, וְקֵרְבָנוּ לִפְנֵי הַר סִינַי, וְנָתַן לָנוּ אֶת הַתּוֹרָה, וְהִכְנִיסָנוּ לְאֶרֶץ יִשְׂרָאֵל, וּבָנָה לָנוּ אֶת בֵּית הַבְּחִירָה לְכַפֵּר עַל כָּל עֲוֹנוֹתֵינוּ.

HISTORY

DID YOU KNOW?

Q How can we say "had Hashem fed us the *mann* but had not given us the mitzvah of Shabbos," if we know that B'nei Yisrael received the mitzvah of Shabbos in Marah, *before* they started getting *mann* (in Alush)?

A Some say that the laws of Shabbos were actually given in Alush, when B'nei Yisrael began receiving the *mann*.

Others answer that although Hashem gave the laws of Shabbos in Marah, Moshe Rabbeinu did not pass them onto B'nei Yisrael until they were in Alush.

Q What would have been the point of bringing us to Har Sinai if we would not have received the Torah?

A There are many answers to this question, including:

1. The phrase means that if we would have received just the Aseres Hadibros that were said at Har Sinai, even if we didn't receive the rest of the Torah, it would have been enough.

2. Or it means that if we would have experienced the great revelation of Hashem that occurred at Har Sinai, but not received the Torah, it would have been enough for us.

If He had supplied our needs in the desert for forty years,
but had not fed us the *mann*
— it would have been reason enough for us to thank Him.

If He had fed us the *mann*,
but had not given us the mitzvah of **Shabbos**
— it would have been reason enough for us to thank Him.

If He had given us the mitzvah of **Shabbos**,
but had not brought us before Har Sinai
— it would have been reason enough for us to thank Him.

If He had brought us before Har Sinai and
only given us the Aseres Hadibros,
but had not given us the rest of the **Torah**
— it would have been reason enough for us to thank Him.

If He had given us the entire **Torah**,
but had not taken us into Eretz Yisrael
— it would have been reason enough for us to thank Him.

If He had taken us into Eretz Yisrael,
but had not built for us His **chosen home,** the Beis Hamikdash
— it would have been reason enough for us to thank Him.

עַל **How much more so** should we be grateful to **Hashem** now that He has done all these things for us and showered **upon us doubled and redoubled goodness —**
He took us out of Egypt. He carried out judgments against the Egyptians and punished **them. He destroyed their gods; He killed their firstborn. He gave us their wealth. He split the sea for us. He took us through it on** completely **dry land. He drowned our enemies in it. He supplied our needs in the desert for forty years; He fed us the** *mann.* **He gave us the** mitzvah of **Shabbos; He brought us before Har Sinai. He gave us the** entire **Torah. He brought us into Eretz Yisrael. And He built for us His chosen Home,** the Beis Hamikdash, so that we could bring korbanos **to atone for all our aveiros.**

רַבָּן גַּמְלִיאֵל הָיָה אוֹמֵר: כָּל שֶׁלֹּא אָמַר שְׁלֹשָׁה דְבָרִים אֵלּוּ בְּפֶסַח לֹא יָצָא יְדֵי חוֹבָתוֹ. וְאֵלּוּ הֵן:

פֶּסַח, מַצָּה וּמָרוֹר.

פֶּסַח שֶׁהָיוּ אֲבוֹתֵינוּ אוֹכְלִים בִּזְמַן שֶׁבֵּית הַמִּקְדָּשׁ קַיָּם עַל שׁוּם מָה, עַל שׁוּם שֶׁפָּסַח הַמָּקוֹם עַל בָּתֵּי אֲבוֹתֵינוּ בְּמִצְרַיִם, שֶׁנֶּאֱמַר: וַאֲמַרְתֶּם זֶבַח פֶּסַח הוּא לַיָי אֲשֶׁר פָּסַח עַל בָּתֵּי בְנֵי יִשְׂרָאֵל בְּמִצְרַיִם בְּנָגְפּוֹ אֶת מִצְרַיִם וְאֶת בָּתֵּינוּ הִצִּיל, וַיִּקֹּד הָעָם וַיִּשְׁתַּחֲווּ.

רַבָּן Rabban Gamliel used to say: Whoever has not discussed the reasons for the following three things on Pesach has not properly fulfilled his obligation of Sippur Yetzias Mitzrayim.

They are:

The Korban Pesach, Matzah, and Marror.

פֶּסַח What is the reason for the Korban called "Korban Pesach" which our ancestors ate in the times of the Beis Hamikdash?

The Korban Pesach was offered because the word "pesach" means to "pass over," and Hashem passed over our ancestors' houses in Egypt and spared their firstborn. As it says in the Torah: You should say to your son, "This is a Korban Pesach for Hashem, because He *passed over* the houses of B'nei Yisrael in Egypt when He struck the Egyptians' firstborn, and He spared our households." Then B'nei Yisrael bent their knees, and bowed down to Hashem.

 DID YOU KNOW?

 NUSACH

In the Torah, Hashem calls the Yom Tov "Chag Hamatzos," to show **our** greatness—that we trusted Hashem and rushed out of Mitzrayim; we didn't even wait long enough to let the dough rise. We, on the other hand, call the Yom Tov "Pesach," to show **Hashem's** greatness—that He "passed over" our houses when punishing the Mitzrim.

Q Does one fulfill the mitzvah of Sippur Yetzias Mitzrayim properly just by saying the words "Pesach," "Matzah," and "Marror?"

A No. In order to fulfill the mitzvah properly, one must also explain the reasons for the Korban Pesach, matzah, and marror.

נוֹטֵל הַפְּרוּסָה בְּיָדוֹ וְיֹאמַר:

Hold on to the second and third matzah (leaving them in the matzah cover) while reading the purple text.

מַצָּה זוֹ שֶׁאָנוּ אוֹכְלִים עַל שׁוּם מָה, עַל שׁוּם שֶׁלֹּא הִסְפִּיק בְּצֵקֶת שֶׁל אֲבוֹתֵינוּ לְהַחֲמִיץ עַד שֶׁנִּגְלָה עֲלֵיהֶם מֶלֶךְ מַלְכֵי הַמְּלָכִים הַקָּדוֹשׁ בָּרוּךְ הוּא וּגְאָלָם, שֶׁנֶּאֱמַר: וַיֹּאפוּ אֶת הַבָּצֵק אֲשֶׁר הוֹצִיאוּ מִמִּצְרַיִם עֻגֹת מַצּוֹת, כִּי לֹא חָמֵץ, כִּי גֹרְשׁוּ מִמִּצְרַיִם וְלֹא יָכְלוּ לְהִתְמַהְמֵהַּ, וְגַם צֵדָה לֹא עָשׂוּ לָהֶם.

נוֹטֵל הַמָּרוֹר בְּיָדוֹ וְיֹאמַר:

Place one hand on each of the marror portions on the kaarah while reading the purple text.

מָרוֹר זֶה שֶׁאָנוּ אוֹכְלִים עַל שׁוּם מָה, עַל שׁוּם שֶׁמֵּרְרוּ הַמִּצְרִים אֶת חַיֵּי אֲבוֹתֵינוּ בְּמִצְרָיִם, שֶׁנֶּאֱמַר: וַיְמָרְרוּ אֶת חַיֵּיהֶם בַּעֲבֹדָה קָשָׁה בְּחֹמֶר וּבִלְבֵנִים וּבְכָל עֲבֹדָה בַּשָּׂדֶה, אֵת כָּל עֲבֹדָתָם אֲשֶׁר עָבְדוּ בָהֶם בְּפָרֶךְ.

 **HISTORY**

The speed with which B'nei Yisrael left Egypt was crucial to the redemption. For, if they had remained in Egypt for one more instant, they would never have been redeemed.

 DID YOU KNOW?

The prohibition to eat chametz when B'nei Yisrael left Mitzrayim was only for that night and the following day, and not for seven days as it is now. Therefore, had they not been in a rush to leave on that day, they would have indeed let their dough rise into chametz on the following days.

 **WORD POWER**

Q When we describe Hashem as the מֶלֶךְ מַלְכֵי הַמְּלָכִים — "King over the kings of kings," to which kings is it referring?

A The basic "kings" are the human kings.

The "kings of kings" are the angels who rule and control the human kings.

Hashem is the King over them all.

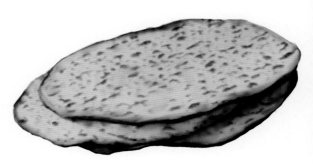

מַצָּה **What is the reason for the** matzah **that we eat?**

We eat matzah **because the dough of our ancestors did not have enough time to rise before** Hashem, **the King over the kings of kings, revealed Himself to them and redeemed them** from Egypt. **As it says** in the Torah regarding Yetzias Mitzrayim: **They baked the dough they had taken out of Egypt** into **round matzos, because it had not risen, since they were chased out of Egypt and could not wait** for the dough to rise. They were in such a rush that **they also did not** have enough time to **prepare any** other **provisions** for the way.

מָרוֹר **What is the reason for the** marror **that we eat?**

We eat marror **because the Egyptians** made the lives of our fathers in **Egypt bitter. As it says** in the Torah: **They made their lives bitter with hard work** – by making them work **with mortar and bricks and all** kinds of **work in the fields. All their work that the Egyptians** made them do was **backbreaking work.**

A DEEPER LOOK

Q The Mishnah says that the reason we eat matzah is simply because our ancestors were redeemed from Egypt. What is gained by the Haggadah describing the great speed with which they were redeemed?

A With just the explanation in the Mishnah, we could have been commanded to eat **any** food as a commemoration of Yetzias Mitzrayim.

By describing the great speed with which Yetzias Mitzrayim happened—that there wasn't even time for the dough to rise—the Haggadah is explaining why we should specifically eat **matzah** to commemorate Yetzias Mitzrayim.

SEDER OF THE SEDER

Q If the reason for eating matzah is to commemorate the rush in which they left Egypt, why did Hashem command B'nei Yisrael to eat matzah with the Korban Pesach on the night *before* they left Egypt?

A Hashem knew that they would leave in a rush the next day, and their dough would not have time to rise. He commanded them to eat matzah on the night before they left, in commemoration of the hurried escape that He would bring about the next day.

בְּכָל דּוֹר וָדוֹר

חַיָּב אָדָם לִרְאוֹת אֶת עַצְמוֹ
כְּאִלּוּ הוּא יָצָא מִמִּצְרַיִם,

שֶׁנֶּאֱמַר: וְהִגַּדְתָּ לְבִנְךָ בַּיּוֹם הַהוּא לֵאמֹר בַּעֲבוּר זֶה עָשָׂה יְיָ לִי בְּצֵאתִי מִמִּצְרָיִם. לֹא אֶת אֲבוֹתֵינוּ בִּלְבָד גָּאַל הַקָּדוֹשׁ בָּרוּךְ הוּא מִמִּצְרַיִם, אֶלָּא אַף אוֹתָנוּ גָּאַל עִמָּהֶם, שֶׁנֶּאֱמַר: וְאוֹתָנוּ הוֹצִיא מִשָּׁם לְמַעַן הָבִיא אוֹתָנוּ לָתֶת לָנוּ אֶת הָאָרֶץ אֲשֶׁר נִשְׁבַּע לַאֲבוֹתֵינוּ.

בְּכָל In each and every generation, and on each and every day, **a person must see himself as if he had** personally **left Egypt** on that day.

As it says in the Torah: **You should tell your son on that** distant **day**—even many generations later, **"Hashem did** miracles **for** *me* **when** *I* **left Egypt** in order that I keep His mitzvos, such as **these** mitzvos of Korban Pesach, and eating matzah and marror." **Hashem redeemed not only our ancestors from Egypt, but also redeemed us** along with them. **As it says** in the Torah: Hashem **took us out of Egypt in order to bring us to the land** He promised to our ancestors, and to give it to us.

DID YOU KNOW?

Q How often must the people in "every generation" see themselves as if they personally came out of Mitzrayim?

A A person must think every day: Not just my ancestors, but I was also saved from being in Mitzrayim today!

יְכַסֶּה אֶת הַפַּת וְיַגְבִּיהַּ אֶת הַכּוֹס וְאוֹחֲזוֹ בְּיָדוֹ עַד סִיּוּם בִּרְכַּת אֲשֶׁר גְּאָלָנוּ:

Cover the matzos and hold the cup as during
Kiddush while saying the following:

לְפִיכָךְ אֲנַחְנוּ חַיָּבִים לְהוֹדוֹת לְהַלֵּל לְשַׁבֵּחַ לְפָאֵר לְרוֹמֵם
לְהַדֵּר לְבָרֵךְ לְעַלֵּה וּלְקַלֵּס, לְמִי שֶׁעָשָׂה לַאֲבוֹתֵינוּ
וְלָנוּ אֶת כָּל הַנִּסִּים הָאֵלּוּ. הוֹצִיאָנוּ מֵעַבְדוּת לְחֵרוּת, מִיָּגוֹן
לְשִׂמְחָה, וּמֵאֵבֶל לְיוֹם טוֹב, וּמֵאֲפֵלָה לְאוֹר גָּדוֹל, וּמִשִּׁעְבּוּד
לִגְאֻלָּה, וְנֹאמַר לְפָנָיו הַלְלוּיָהּ.

Place the cup on the table.

הַלְלוּיָהּ, הַלְלוּ עַבְדֵי יְיָ, הַלְלוּ אֶת שֵׁם יְיָ. יְהִי שֵׁם יְיָ מְבֹרָךְ,
מֵעַתָּה וְעַד עוֹלָם. מִמִּזְרַח שֶׁמֶשׁ עַד מְבוֹאוֹ,
מְהֻלָּל שֵׁם יְיָ. רָם עַל כָּל גּוֹיִם יְיָ, עַל הַשָּׁמַיִם כְּבוֹדוֹ. מִי כַּיְיָ
אֱלֹהֵינוּ, הַמַּגְבִּיהִי לָשָׁבֶת. הַמַּשְׁפִּילִי לִרְאוֹת, בַּשָּׁמַיִם וּבָאָרֶץ.
מְקִימִי מֵעָפָר דָּל, מֵאַשְׁפֹּת יָרִים אֶבְיוֹן. לְהוֹשִׁיבִי עִם נְדִיבִים,
עִם נְדִיבֵי עַמּוֹ. מוֹשִׁיבִי עֲקֶרֶת הַבַּיִת, אֵם הַבָּנִים שְׂמֵחָה,
הַלְלוּיָהּ.

MINHAGIM

The minhag of the Rebbeim was
to lift the cup and hold it until
the words וְנֹאמַר לְפָנָיו הַלְלוּיָהּ at the
end of the paragraph. They would
then rest the cup on the table, and
lift it again for the brachah of אֲשֶׁר
גְּאָלָנוּ (page 90).

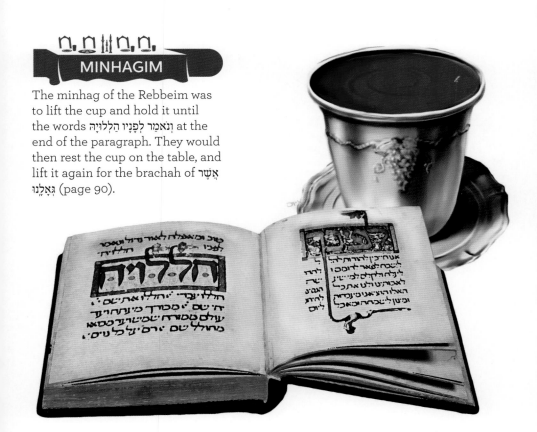

לְפִיכָךְ **Therefore we must thank, laud, praise, glorify, exalt, adore, bless, elevate, and honor** Hashem, **Who did all these miracles for our ancestors and for us. He took us out from slavery to freedom, from sorrow to joy, from mourning to a day of celebration, from darkness to great light, and from slavery to redemption. Let us therefore declare before Him: "Praise Hashem."**

הַלְלוּיָהּ **Everyone should praise Hashem. Servants of Hashem,** give **praise. Praise the name of Hashem. May Hashem's name be blessed** by all creations, **now and forever. From** the people who live in the east where the **sun rises, to** the people who live in the west where **it sets, Hashem's name is praised. Hashem is** in the heavens, **high above all the nations** of the world. **Hashem's glory is above the heavens. Who is like Hashem, our God, Who,** even though He **rests up high** above the world, still **lowers Himself to look** down **upon the heaven and earth** and keeps them in existence. **He picks up** a **needy** person **from** the **dust** of poverty, and **He lifts** a **poor** person **from the garbage.** Not only does Hashem take poor people out of poverty, He raises them **to** a position where they can **sit with noblemen; with the noblemen of His nation,** B'nei Yisrael. Hashem **settles a woman who cannot** naturally **have children into a house;** He gives her many children. He makes her **a happy mother of children. Praise Hashem.**

WORD POWER

Starting from "lehodos," we use ten different words of praise. The last one, "hallelukah," is the greatest of them all because it combines one of Hashem's names (י - ה) with praise of Him (הלל).

HISTORY

We say Hallel during the Seder just as B'nei Yisrael sang Hallel when they left Egypt.

NUSACH

Q Why don't we say the brachah "לִקְרוֹא אֶת הַהַלֵּל" like we normally do before saying Hallel?

A There are many reasons for this, including:

- We do not say a brachah on a mitzvah that is not completed all at once. Because we interrupt Hallel—by eating the matzah and marror, eating the meal and saying Birkas Hamazon—we do not say a brachah before saying it.

- We are not saying Hallel to fulfill the mitzvah, as we do during davening. We're just singing songs of praise to Hashem from the perakim in Tehillim that make up Hallel.

בְּצֵאת

יִשְׂרָאֵל מִמִּצְרַיִם,

בֵּית יַעֲקֹב מֵעַם לֹעֵז.

הָיְתָה יְהוּדָה לְקָדְשׁוּ, יִשְׂרָאֵל מַמְשְׁלוֹתָיו.

הַיָּם רָאָה וַיָּנֹס, הַיַּרְדֵּן יִסֹּב לְאָחוֹר.

הֶהָרִים רָקְדוּ כְאֵילִים, גְּבָעוֹת כִּבְנֵי צֹאן.

מַה לְּךָ הַיָּם כִּי תָנוּס, הַיַּרְדֵּן תִּסֹּב לְאָחוֹר.

הֶהָרִים תִּרְקְדוּ כְאֵילִים, גְּבָעוֹת כִּבְנֵי צֹאן.

מִלִּפְנֵי אָדוֹן חוּלִי אָרֶץ, מִלִּפְנֵי אֱלוֹהַּ יַעֲקֹב.

הַהֹפְכִי הַצּוּר אֲגַם מָיִם, חַלָּמִישׁ לְמַעְיְנוֹ מָיִם.

DID YOU KNOW?

Q Why don't we stand when saying Hallel here, as we usually do?

A Everything we do tonight is performed with a sense of freedom and royalty. Therefore, we sit during Hallel instead of standing.

SEDER OF THE SEDER

Q Why do we split Hallel in two parts—one part during Maggid, and the other after Birkas Hamazon?

A The part of Hallel we say during Maggid, "Hallelukah" and "B'tzeis Yisrael"—discusses things that have **already** happened, Yetzias Mitzrayim and Krias Yam Suf. We then interrupt to say the brachah "אֲשֶׁר גְּאָלָנוּ," in which we thank Hashem for these things.

The rest of Hallel discusses things that will happen in the **future**—when Moshiach comes.

בְּצֵאת When B'nei Yisrael went out of Egypt,
when **the House of Yaakov** went out **from** among **a nation** that spoke a foreign language,

the people of **Yehudah became His holy** nation; B'nei **Yisrael** came under His rulership.

The Yam Suf **saw** B'nei Yisrael coming, **and it fled** so that B'nei Yisrael could walk through. During that time, all the waters of the world split, including **the Yarden** river, which **turned** and flowed **backwards**.

When Hashem's glory was revealed at Har Sinai during Matan Torah, the world shook and **the mountains skipped like rams. The** nearby **hills** skipped **like young sheep.**

What is with **you,** Yam Suf; why is it **that you run?** Why is it, **Yarden** river, that **you turn** and flow **backwards?**

What is with you **mountains,** that **you skip like rams,** and what is with **the hills** that skip **like young sheep?**

The sea, the mountains, and the hills answer: We do this in awe of being **before the Master,** Hashem, **the Creator of the earth;** we are **before** Hashem, **the God of Yaakov,**

Who turns the rock into a pool of water and Who turns **the flint stone into a fountain of water.** When B'nei Yisrael needed water in the desert, Hashem turned a rock into a fountain of water.

Hold the cup in the same manner as during
Kiddush and say the following two brachos:

בָּרוּךְ אַתָּה יְיָ, אֱלֹהֵינוּ מֶלֶךְ הָעוֹלָם, אֲשֶׁר גְּאָלָנוּ
וְגָאַל אֶת אֲבוֹתֵינוּ מִמִּצְרַיִם, וְהִגִּיעָנוּ הַלַּיְלָה
הַזֶּה לֶאֱכָל בּוֹ מַצָּה וּמָרוֹר, כֵּן יְיָ אֱלֹהֵינוּ וֵאלֹהֵי
אֲבוֹתֵינוּ יַגִּיעֵנוּ לְמוֹעֲדִים וְלִרְגָלִים אֲחֵרִים הַבָּאִים
לִקְרָאתֵנוּ לְשָׁלוֹם, שְׂמֵחִים בְּבִנְיַן עִירֶךָ, וְשָׂשִׂים
בַּעֲבוֹדָתֶךָ, וְנֹאכַל שָׁם

On Motza'ei Shabbos: On all nights except Motza'ei Shabbos:
מִן הַפְּסָחִים וּמִן הַזְּבָחִים   מִן הַזְּבָחִים וּמִן הַפְּסָחִים

אֲשֶׁר יַגִּיעַ דָּמָם עַל קִיר מִזְבַּחֲךָ לְרָצוֹן, וְנוֹדֶה לְךָ
שִׁיר חָדָשׁ עַל גְּאֻלָתֵנוּ וְעַל פְּדוּת נַפְשֵׁנוּ. בָּרוּךְ אַתָּה
יְיָ, גָּאַל יִשְׂרָאֵל.

וּמְבָרֵךְ וְשׁוֹתֶה בַּהֲסִבָּה:

בָּרוּךְ אַתָּה יְיָ, אֱלֹהֵינוּ מֶלֶךְ הָעוֹלָם, בּוֹרֵא פְּרִי הַגָּפֶן.

Drink the entire cup (or at least most of it) without
interruption while seated and leaning on the left side.

DID YOU KNOW?

Q How can we say גְאָלָנוּ - that Hashem redeemed *us*, when Yetzias Mitzrayim took place hundreds of years ago?

A If Hashem hadn't saved our ancestors back then, we would have remained slaves in Egypt until this very day, and we would be living there in galus. Therefore, we can truly say that Hashem redeemed **us**.

WORD POWER

Q What's the difference between רְגָלִים and מוֹעֲדִים?

A רְגָלִים are the Yamim Tovim when B'nei Yisrael had the mitzvah to be "oleh regel" (to go up to the Beis Hamikdash), Pesach, Shavuos, and Sukkos. מוֹעֲדִים refer to the other Yamim Tovim, including Rosh Hashanah and Yom Kippur.

בָּרוּךְ Blessed are You, Hashem, our God, King of the world, Who redeemed us and redeemed our ancestors from Egypt, and brought us to this night so that we can fulfill the mitzvos to eat matzah and marror.

So too, Hashem, our God and the God of our fathers, bring us to celebrate other holidays (Rosh Hashanah and Yom Kippur) and Yamim Tovim (Pesach, Shavuos, and Sukkos) that are coming to us in peace with the coming of Moshiach, when we will rejoice in the rebuilding of Your city, Yerushalayim, and we will be joyful in serving You in the Beis Hamikdash. Then we will eat of the Korbanos Chagigah and Korbanos Pesach, whose blood will be sprinkled on the side of Your Mizbei'ach so that they should be accepted.

We will then sing a new song to thank You for redeeming us and for redeeming our neshamos from this galus.

Blessed are You, Hashem, Who redeemed B'nei Yisrael from Egypt.

Blessed are You, Hashem, our God, King of the world, Who creates the fruit of the vine.

SEDER OF THE SEDER

Q Why do we change the order in which we mention the two korbanos on Motza'ei Shabbos?

A In the times of the Beis Hamikdash, when Erev Pesach occurred on a weekday, the Korban Chagigah was eaten before the Korban Pesach, because the Korban Pesach should be eaten when the person is no longer hungry. Therefore the Chagigah is mentioned first.

However, the Korban Chagigah could not be offered on Shabbos (since it could be offered during the next several days). Therefore, when Erev Pesach occurred on a Shabbos, the Korban Pesach, which was eaten on the first night of Pesach, was eaten before the Korban Chagigah, which was offered and eaten the next day.

NUSACH

Each of the four cups is considered an individual mitzvah on its own, and therefore needs its own brachah of "Hagafen." However, the brachah achronah is an inclusive brachah said after finishing to eat and drink. Therefore it is said only once, at the end of the Seder, for all four cups of wine.

רָחְצָה

Review the five steps of רָחְצָה through כּוֹרֵךְ at this point, to avoid making an interruption between them.

וְאַחַר כָּךְ נוֹטֵל יָדָיו וּמְבָרֵךְ עַל נְטִילַת יָדָיִם:

Wash your hands in the following manner:

- Pick up the cup containing the water in your right hand. Pass it to your left hand, and pour three times on your right hand. Then pass the cup to your right hand and pour three times on your left hand. (It is customary to hold the cup with a towel when pouring.)

- A little water from the final pouring should remain in your left hand. Rub this water over both hands together, while saying the following brachah:

בָּרוּךְ אַתָּה יְיָ, אֱלֹהֵינוּ מֶלֶךְ הָעוֹלָם, אֲשֶׁר קִדְּשָׁנוּ בְּמִצְוֹתָיו, וְצִוָּנוּ עַל נְטִילַת יָדָיִם.

בָּרוּךְ **Blessed are You, Hashem, our God, King of the world, Who made us holy with His mitzvos and commanded us** through the Chachamim **regarding washing** our **hands** before eating bread.

Dry your hands completely. Do not talk from this point until after eating the matzah (preferably until after eating the Korech "sandwich").

DID YOU KNOW?

Matzah is referred to in the Zohar as מֵיכְלָא דִמְהֵימְנוּתָא - food that strengthens our emunah and מֵיכְלָא דְאַסְוָותָא - food that heals.

The Alter Rebbe said that more specifically, the matzah of the first night strengthens our emunah, and matzah of the second night heals. This order shows that ideally, a person's emunah should cause the healing, rather than the healing causing the emunah.

- Each participant is required to eat at least a kezayis of matzah. Since it is impossible for everyone to receive the required amount from the two matzos of the kaarah, other matzos should be available. However, it is preferable that all receive at least a small piece of the two matzos of the kaarah.

- Each kezayis is approximately half of a shmurah matzah.

- The entire amount should be eaten within approximately four to seven minutes.

- One should not speak of anything unrelated to the Seder until after eating the Korech.

- The matzah is not dipped in salt.

See further instructions for Motzi on page 94.

A DEEPER LOOK

Q Why do we hold the two whole matzos and the broken piece while we say the brachah of Hamotzi?

A There are many answers, including:

- As it is on any Yom Tov, we must say the brachah Hamotzi on lechem mishneh, so we have the two whole matzos. We add the broken piece so that we have "lechem oni," poor bread as well.

- Some opinions say that the brachah of Hamotzi should be said on the broken piece, while others say it should be said on the whole matzos. To make sure we are doing it right according to both opinions, we hold all three matzos in our hand when we say the brachah.

NUSACH

Q Why don't we say the brachah of "Shehecheyanu" for the mitzvah of eating matzah?

A We already said a form of Shehecheyanu in the brachah "אֲשֶׁר גְּאָלָנוּ," when we said the words וְהִגִּיעָנוּ הַלַּיְלָה הַזֶּה לֶאֱכָל בּוֹ מַצָּה וּמָרוֹר.

SEDER OF THE SEDER

Q Why do we say the brachah of "Hamotzi" *before* "Al achilas matzah?"

A The general rule is תָּדִיר וְשֶׁאֵינוֹ תָּדִיר – תָּדִיר קוֹדֶם, if there are two mitzvos that need to be done, the more common one is done first. We say "Hamotzi" far more often than we fulfill the mitzvah of eating matzah, and therefore say "Hamotzi" first.

STORY

The Baal Shem Tov heard the following from Achiyah Hashiloni, and told it to the Mezritcher Maggid, who told it to the Alter Rebbe and it has been passed on to every Rebbe since, and repeated by each of them: Matzah is known as מִכְלָא דִמְהֵימְנוּתָא (food of faith) and מִכְלָא דְאַסְוָותָא (food of health) because it strengthens and heals our emunah (belief) in Hashem.

וְיִקַּח הַמַּצּוֹת כְּסֵדֶר שֶׁהִנִּיחָם הַפְּרוּסָה בֵּין שְׁתֵּי הַשְּׁלֵמוֹת וְיֹאחֲזֵם בְּיָדוֹ וִיבָרֵךְ:

Hold the three matzos (while still covered
by the cloth) and say the following:

בָּרוּךְ אַתָּה יְיָ, אֱלֹהֵינוּ מֶלֶךְ הָעוֹלָם, הַמּוֹצִיא לֶחֶם מִן הָאָרֶץ.

בָּרוּךְ Blessed are You, Hashem, our God, King of the world, Who brings
forth grain **out of the earth** so that we can make **bread**.

Do not break the matzos until after saying the next brachah.

וְלֹא יִבְצַע מֵהֶן אֶלָּא יַנִּיחַ הַמַּצָּה הַשְּׁלִישִׁית לְהִשָּׁמֵט מִיָּדוֹ וִיבָרֵךְ עַל הַפְּרוּסָה עִם הָעֶלְיוֹנָה טֶרֶם יִשְׁבְּרֵם בְּרָכָה זוֹ. וִיכַוֵּן לִפְטוֹר גַּם כֵּן אֲכִילַת הַכְּרִיכָה שֶׁמִּמַּצָּה הַשְּׁלִישִׁית וְגַם אֲכִילַת הָאֲפִיקוֹמָן יִפְטוֹר בִּבְרָכָה זוֹ:

Let go of the bottom matzah and say the following brachah.

Bear in mind that it also applies to the eating of the "sandwich" of Korech—
which will be made with the third (bottom) matzah—and also to the eating of the
Afikoman at the end of the meal.

בָּרוּךְ אַתָּה יְיָ, אֱלֹהֵינוּ מֶלֶךְ הָעוֹלָם, אֲשֶׁר קִדְּשָׁנוּ בְּמִצְוֹתָיו, וְצִוָּנוּ עַל אֲכִילַת מַצָּה.

בָּרוּךְ Blessed are You, Hashem, our God, King of the world, Who made
us holy with His mitzvos and commanded us regarding eating matzah
on Pesach.

וְאַחַר כָּךְ יִבְצַע כַּזַּיִת מִכָּל אֶחָד מִשְׁתֵּיהֶן וְיֹאכְלֵם בְּיַחַד בַּהֲסִבָּה:

Break off a kezayis from each of the top two matzos, and eat
the two pieces together while leaning on your left side.

A DEEPER LOOK

Even nowadays, the mitzvah
of eating matzah is a mitzvah
Min Hatorah, for both men and
women.

MINHAGIM

Q Why don't we dip the matzah into salt?

A The mitzvah of matzah is so
special that we do not want to mix
any other taste into it.

מָרוֹר

וְאַחַר כָּךְ יִקַּח כְּזַיִת מָרוֹר וְיִטְבֹּל בַּחֲרֹסֶת וִינַעֵר הַחֲרֹסֶת מֵעָלָיו כְּדֵי שֶׁלֹּא יִתְבַּטֵּל טַעַם הַמְּרִירוּת וִיבָרֵךְ בְּרָכָה זוֹ:

- Soften the charoses with wine.
- Take at least a kezayis of marror from the kaarah and dip it into the charoses.

- Shake off the charoses so that the bitter taste of the marror will not be nullified.
- When saying the following brachah, bear in mind that it is also for the chazeres of the "sandwich" of Korech.

בָּרוּךְ אַתָּה יְיָ, אֱלֹהֵינוּ מֶלֶךְ הָעוֹלָם, אֲשֶׁר קִדְּשָׁנוּ בְּמִצְוֹתָיו, וְצִוָּנוּ עַל אֲכִילַת מָרוֹר.

בָּרוּךְ **Blessed are You, Hashem, our God, King of the world, Who made us holy with His mitzvos and commanded us about eating marror** on Pesach.

וְיֹאכְלֶנּוּ בְּלֹא הֲסִבָּה:

Eat the marror without leaning.

- The entire kezayis should be eaten within approximately four to seven minutes.
- Each participant is required to eat a kezayis of marror. Since it is impossible for everyone to receive the required amount from the marror on the kaarah, other marror should be available.

SEDER OF THE SEDER

NUSACH

To make sure that there is no interruption between saying the brachah on marror and eating it, we dip the marror into charoses before saying the brachah.

Q The Chachamim decreed that we must eat charoses with the marror. Why don't we say a separate brachah on the mitzvah of eating charoses?

A Charoses helps to remind us of the hard work—building with cement and bricks—which made B'nei Yisrael's lives bitter. It is therefore part of the mitzvah of marror, and does not need its own brachah.

וְאַחַר כָּךְ יִקַּח מַצָּה הַג' וַחֲזֶרֶת עִמָּהּ כְּשִׁעוּר כַּזַּיִת וְיִטְבֹּל בַּחֲרֹסֶת וְיִכְרְכֵם בְּיַחַד וְיֹאמַר זֶה:

Take a kezayis of the third matzah and a kezayis of the chazeres. Place some dry charoses on the chazeres and then shake it off. Combine the two—like a sandwich—and say the following:

כֵּן עָשָׂה הִלֵּל בִּזְמַן שֶׁבֵּית הַמִּקְדָּשׁ הָיָה קַיָּם, הָיָה כּוֹרֵךְ פֶּסַח מַצָּה וּמָרוֹר וְאוֹכֵל בְּיַחַד, כְּמוֹ שֶׁנֶּאֱמַר: עַל מַצּוֹת וּמְרוֹרִים יֹאכְלֻהוּ.

כֵּן **The following is what Hillel used to do in the times of the Beis Hamikdash: He would combine the** Korban **Pesach, matzah, and marror and eat them together. As it says** in the Torah: **They should eat** the Korban Pesach **with matzah and marror.**

וְיֹאכְלֵם בְּיַחַד [וּבַהֲסִבָּה. טוּר וְשֻׁלְחָן עָרוּךְ סִימָן תע"ה. הַגָּהָה מִסִּדּוּר אַדְמוֹ"ר בַּעַל צֶמַח צֶדֶק זִכְרוֹנוֹ לִבְרָכָה]:

Eat the Korech "sandwich" while leaning on the left side.

- The Korech should be eaten within approximately four to seven minutes.
- Each participant is required to eat a kezayis of matzah and a kezayis of chazeres. Since it is impossible for everyone to receive the required amount from the matzah and chazeres of the kaarah, other matzos and chazeres should be available.

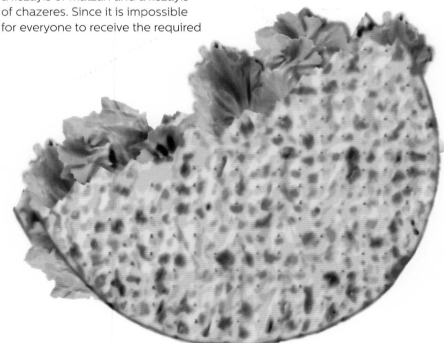

WORD POWER

Q How can we say, "בֵּן עָשָׂה הָלֵּל," that *this* Korech sandwich we are holding is like the one Hillel would make, when nowadays we do not include the meat of the Korban Pesach as Hillel did?

A There are many answers to this, including:

- The word "בֵּן" is not referring to what we are doing now at the Seder, but rather to the continuation of the paragraph, which describes how Hillel would make his Korech sandwich.

- We are pointing out that our sandwich is similar to Hillel's in that they both include matzah and marror.

HISTORY

We eat Korech as a reminder of what Hillel would do. He would dip the Korech into charoses and eat it while leaning. Therefore we do the same when eating our Korech.

DID YOU KNOW?

עָשָׂה הָלֵּל בִּזְמַן
שֶׁבֵּית הַמִּקְדָּשׁ הָיָה קַיָם

These words don't mean that Hillel only did it during the part of his life when the Beis Hamikdash was still standing, because in fact, the Beis Hamikdash was standing during Hillel's entire lifetime.

The Haggadah is explaining the reason why Hillel was able to make his Korech sandwich with the Korban Pesach—because the Beis Hamikdash was standing.

A DEEPER LOOK

Q Why is it necessary to eat the matzah by itself, the marror by itself, and then to eat them together in the Korech sandwich?

A Matzah must be eaten alone because eating marror with it would cancel its taste.

Regarding marror, there is a machlokes whether it should be eaten alone, or—according to Hillel—together with matzah (and also the Korban Pesach, in the times of the Beis Hamikdash). In order to fulfill the mitzvah according to both opinions, we eat it both alone, and together with matzah.

וְאַחַר כָּךְ אוֹכֵל וְשׁוֹתֶה כְּדֵי צָרְכּוֹ וְיָכוֹל לִשְׁתּוֹת יַיִן בֵּין כּוֹס ב׳ לְג׳:

Eat the Yom Tov meal.

- Begin the meal by eating a hard boiled egg dipped in salt water. (Those who have a kaarah use the egg from there.)

- Minhag Chabad is not to lean while eating the meal.

- Eat enough so that you will be satisfied before eating the Afikoman. (The Afikoman commemorates the Korban Pesach, which was to be eaten when satisfied.) However, do not overeat so that you would not have any appetite at all for the Afikoman.

- On the first night, make sure that you have enough time to eat the Afikoman before chatzos (midnight).

MINHAGIM

Minhag Chabad is to be very careful about gebrokts (getting matzah wet) throughout the Yom Tov, except for Acharon shel Pesach. To prevent matzah from becoming wet:

- We keep any matzah on the table covered so that no liquid will drip on it.

- Before pouring water into any vessel, it should be checked to ensure there are no crumbs of matzah in it.

- We do not wipe our wet fingers over the lips when washing mayim achronim, in case there are crumbs of matzah there.

SEDER OF THE SEDER

Q Why do we eat the Afikoman before chatzos on the first night?

A Because it is eaten in place of the Korban Pesach, which had to be eaten before chatzos.

DID YOU KNOW?

Q Why is an egg eaten during this meal?

A An egg is a symbol of mourning. We mourn the destruction of the Beis Hamikdash and the fact that we are unable to offer and eat the Korban Pesach.

וְאַחַר כָּךְ יִקַּח הָאֲפִיקוֹמָן וִיחַלְּקוּ לְכָל בְּנֵי בֵיתוֹ לְכָל אֶחָד כַּזַּיִת
וְיִזָּהֵר שֶׁלֹּא יִשְׁתֶּה אַחַר אֲפִיקוֹמָן וְיֹאכַל בַּהֲסִבָּה וְצָרִיךְ לְאָכְלוֹ קֹדֶם חֲצוֹת:

Eat the Afikoman while leaning on the left side.

- The Afikoman should be eaten within approximately four to seven minutes.

- On the first night of Pesach, the Afikoman should be eaten before chatzos (midnight).

- One should not eat or drink anything (even water) after eating the Afikoman for the rest of the night. One should therefore make sure to have had enough liquids so as not to be thirsty after eating the Afikoman.

- Ideally one should at least have some desire to eat while eating the Afikoman, since eating it without any appetite is not the ideal way to fulfill the mitzvah. Nevertheless, one fulfills the obligation even without any appetite.

- There are different opinions as to whether the Afikoman commemorates the Korban Pesach or the matzah that was eaten along with it. Ideally, one should therefore eat two kezeisim of the Afikoman— one kezayis to commemorate the Korban Pesach, and the other kezayis to commemorate the matzah that was eaten along with it. One who finds this too difficult, however, may eat the amount of one kezayis, bearing in mind that this kezayis should serve as a remembrance in accordance with whichever of the two opinions is the correct one (i.e., whether the Afikoman commemorates the Korban Pesach, or the matzah eaten with it).

- Each person receives a piece of the Afikoman. Since it is impossible for everyone to receive the required amount from the matzah put away for the Afikoman, other matzos should be available.

WORD POWER

Q The Alter Rebbe writes that one should "be careful not to drink after the Afikoman." Why did he not simply write, "one should not drink after the Afikoman?"

A The instruction means that one should be careful to drink enough before eating the Afikoman, to ensure that he will not be thirsty and want to drink after eating the Afikoman.

DID YOU KNOW?

Q Why should one not drink anything after eating the Afikoman?

A So that the taste of the Afikoman remains in the mouth.

בָּרֵךְ

וְאַחַר כָּךְ מוֹזְגִין כּוֹס שְׁלִישִׁי וְאוֹמֵר עָלָיו בִּרְכַּת הַמָּזוֹן

The third cup is poured, and Birkas Hamazon is said.
An additional cup, the "Kos Shel Eliyahu," is also filled.

שִׁיר הַמַּעֲלוֹת, בְּשׁוּב יְיָ אֶת שִׁיבַת צִיּוֹן, הָיִינוּ כְּחֹלְמִים. אָז
יִמָּלֵא שְׂחוֹק פִּינוּ וּלְשׁוֹנֵנוּ רִנָּה, אָז יֹאמְרוּ בַגּוֹיִם,
הִגְדִּיל יְיָ לַעֲשׂוֹת עִם אֵלֶּה. הִגְדִּיל יְיָ לַעֲשׂוֹת עִמָּנוּ, הָיִינוּ
שְׂמֵחִים. שׁוּבָה יְיָ אֶת שְׁבִיתֵנוּ, כַּאֲפִיקִים בַּנֶּגֶב. הַזֹּרְעִים
בְּדִמְעָה, בְּרִנָּה יִקְצֹרוּ. הָלוֹךְ יֵלֵךְ וּבָכֹה נֹשֵׂא מֶשֶׁךְ הַזָּרַע, בֹּא
יָבֹא בְרִנָּה נֹשֵׂא אֲלֻמֹּתָיו.

לִבְנֵי קֹרַח מִזְמוֹר שִׁיר, יְסוּדָתוֹ בְּהַרְרֵי קֹדֶשׁ. אֹהֵב יְיָ שַׁעֲרֵי
צִיּוֹן, מִכֹּל מִשְׁכְּנוֹת יַעֲקֹב. נִכְבָּדוֹת מְדֻבָּר בָּךְ, עִיר
הָאֱלֹהִים סֶלָה. אַזְכִּיר רַהַב וּבָבֶל לְיֹדְעָי, הִנֵּה פְלֶשֶׁת וְצוֹר עִם
כּוּשׁ, זֶה יֻלַּד שָׁם. וּלְצִיּוֹן יֵאָמַר אִישׁ וְאִישׁ יֻלַּד בָּהּ, וְהוּא יְכוֹנְנֶהָ
עֶלְיוֹן. יְיָ יִסְפֹּר בִּכְתוֹב עַמִּים, זֶה יֻלַּד שָׁם סֶלָה. וְשָׁרִים כְּחֹלְלִים,
כָּל מַעְיָנַי בָּךְ.

שִׁיר The following is **a song** which was sung by the Levi'im on **the steps in the Beis Hamikdash: When Hashem returns the captured** people of **Tziyon;** when He takes B'nei Yisrael out of galus and returns them to Eretz Yisrael, **we will have been like dreamers.** After Moshiach comes, galus will seem like it was a distant dream that never really happened. **At that time our mouths will be filled with laughter and our tongues** will be filled with **songs** of joy. **The nations** of the world **will say, "Hashem did great** things **for these** people, B'nei Yisrael." B'nei Yisrael will answer the nations, "Yes, **Hashem has done great things for us,** and that is why **we were happy."** While we are in galus, we ask **Hashem,** "Please **return our captives** from galus; may they return quickly to Eretz Yisrael, **like streams of water** flowing quickly **on dry** land, and may all suffering end. When that happens, **those who plant** seeds in these dry places, and are **in tears** because they are afraid no fruit will grow, **will gather** their food **with songs** of happiness. Although he **goes along crying** while **carrying the bag of seeds** in the field, **he will surely come** back to his house **with songs** of happiness, **carrying** all **his bundles** of produce from the field.

לִבְנֵי The following is **a song** that was composed **by the sons of Korach. It is** a song **whose basic** theme **is the holy mountains** of Yerushalayim. **Hashem loves the gates of Tziyon** (Yerushalayim) **more than all the other** parts of Eretz Yisrael in which B'nei **Yisrael live.** Yerushalayim, **glorious** words of Torah **are said** by the Sanhedrin who live **in your gates,** and therefore you will **forever** be called **"the city of Hashem."** When **I mention** and discuss major countries, such as **Egypt, Bavel, Pleshes, Tzor, and Kush with those who know** the greatness of Yerushalayim as **I** do, the other countries do not compare to Yerushalayim's greatness. This is because the other major countries rarely produce a great person; so when people refer to the great person who was born in these countries, they refer to him in the singular form and say, " *This* **person was born there."** However, because Yerushalayim is always full of many great men, when people **speak about Yerushalayim,** they say, "This great **person** *and* that great **person were born there."** Hashem **will establish** Yerushalayim as the most important city **above** all others. When Moshiach comes and **Hashem writes** and decrees destruction on the **nations** that didn't serve Him, He **will count** every Jew and take him out from among the nations, and say, **"This** person's ancestors were **born** in Yerushalayim. He belongs to me!" **Singers as well as musicians** will say, "Yerushalayim, **all my thoughts are about you!"**

אֲבָרְכָה אֶת יְיָ בְּכָל עֵת, תָּמִיד תְּהִלָּתוֹ בְּפִי. סוֹף דָּבָר הַכֹּל נִשְׁמָע, אֶת הָאֱלֹהִים יְרָא וְאֶת מִצְוֹתָיו שְׁמוֹר כִּי זֶה כָּל הָאָדָם. תְּהִלַּת יְיָ יְדַבֶּר פִּי וִיבָרֵךְ כָּל בָּשָׂר שֵׁם קָדְשׁוֹ לְעוֹלָם וָעֶד. וַאֲנַחְנוּ נְבָרֵךְ יָהּ מֵעַתָּה וְעַד עוֹלָם הַלְלוּיָהּ.

קֹדֶם מַיִם אַחֲרוֹנִים יֹאמַר פָּסוּק זֶה:

זֶה חֵלֶק אָדָם רָשָׁע מֵאֱלֹהִים וְנַחֲלַת אִמְרוֹ מֵאֵל.

וְאַחַר מַיִם אַחֲרוֹנִים יֹאמַר פָּסוּק זֶה:

Rinse the fingertips (but do not pass them over the lips as during the rest of the year), then say the following:

וַיְדַבֵּר אֵלַי זֶה הַשֻּׁלְחָן אֲשֶׁר לִפְנֵי יְיָ.

Hold the cup in the same manner as during Kiddush until after the brachah וּבְנֵה on page 106.

When three or more men eat together, one of them leads the rest in Birkas Hamazon. When ten or more eat together, add אֱלֹהֵינוּ as indicated. If there are less then three men at the Seder, continue with בָּרוּךְ, below.

אִם מְבָרְכִין בְּזִמּוּן אוֹמֵר הַמְבָרֵךְ:
Leader

רַבּוֹתַי מִיר וֶועֶלִין בֶּענְטְשִׁין.

וְעוֹנִין הַמְסוּבִּים:
Others & then leader

יְהִי שֵׁם יְיָ מְבֹרָךְ מֵעַתָּה וְעַד עוֹלָם.

הַמְבָרֵךְ אוֹמֵר:
Leader

בִּרְשׁוּת מָרָנָן וְרַבָּנָן וְרַבּוֹתַי נְבָרֵךְ (אֱלֹהֵינוּ) שֶׁאָכַלְנוּ מִשֶּׁלּוֹ.

וְעוֹנִין הַמְסוּבִּים:
Others who have eaten

בָּרוּךְ (אֱלֹהֵינוּ) שֶׁאָכַלְנוּ מִשֶּׁלּוֹ וּבְטוּבוֹ חָיִינוּ.

Leader

בָּרוּךְ (אֱלֹהֵינוּ) שֶׁאָכַלְנוּ מִשֶּׁלּוֹ וּבְטוּבוֹ חָיִינוּ.

בָּרוּךְ אַתָּה יְיָ אֱלֹהֵינוּ מֶלֶךְ הָעוֹלָם, הַזָּן אֶת הָעוֹלָם כֻּלּוֹ בְּטוּבוֹ בְּחֵן בְּחֶסֶד וּבְרַחֲמִים הוּא נוֹתֵן לֶחֶם לְכָל בָּשָׂר כִּי לְעוֹלָם חַסְדּוֹ. וּבְטוּבוֹ הַגָּדוֹל עִמָּנוּ תָּמִיד לֹא חָסַר לָנוּ וְאַל יֶחְסַר לָנוּ מָזוֹן לְעוֹלָם וָעֶד. בַּעֲבוּר שְׁמוֹ הַגָּדוֹל כִּי הוּא אֵל זָן וּמְפַרְנֵס לַכֹּל וּמֵטִיב לַכֹּל וּמֵכִין מָזוֹן לְכָל בְּרִיּוֹתָיו אֲשֶׁר בָּרָא, כָּאָמוּר: פּוֹתֵחַ אֶת יָדֶךָ וּמַשְׂבִּיעַ לְכָל חַי רָצוֹן. בָּרוּךְ אַתָּה יְיָ, הַזָּן אֶת הַכֹּל.

אֲבָרְכָה I will bless Hashem at all times; His praise is always in my mouth. After all is said and heard, fear Hashem and keep His mitzvos, because this is a person's whole purpose in this world. My mouth will say the praises of Hashem, and everyone will do the same and bless His holy name forever and ever. We will bless Hashem now and forever. Praise Hashem.

זֶה All these punishments (mentioned in the pessukim before this passuk in Iyov) are the portion Hashem will give a wicked person, and the heritage Hashem will give to those who speak badly of Him.

וַיְדַבֵּר Yechezkel said: The malach showing me the third Beis Hamikdash, pointed out the Shulchan, and said to me, "This table that you see here before Hashem's Kodesh Hakadashim is the Shulchan."

רַבּוֹתַי Gentlemen, we will bentch.

יְהִי Hashem's name should be blessed from now until forever.

בִּרְשׁוּת With the permission of the Torah scholars, Rabbis, and my teachers here, let us bless Him (our God), Whose food we have eaten from.

בָּרוּךְ Blessed be Hashem (our God), Whose food we have eaten from, and by Whose goodness we live.

בָּרוּךְ Blessed be Hashem (our God), Whose food we have eaten from, and by Whose goodness we live.

בָּרוּךְ Blessed are You, Hashem, our God, King of the world, Who, in His goodness, provides food for the entire world with graciousness, with kindness, and with mercy. He gives food to all of the world's creations, because His kindness lasts forever. Through His great goodness, which is always with us, we do not lack food, and may we never lack food. Hashem gives the world food because of His great name; because He is the God Who provides food and livelihood to everyone. He does good to everyone and He prepares food for all His creations; for everything that He created. As it says in Tehillim: You open Your hand and give enough food to satisfy the desires of every living thing. Blessed are You, Hashem, Who provides food for everyone.

נוֹדֶה לְךָ יְיָ אֱלֹהֵינוּ עַל שֶׁהִנְחַלְתָּ לַאֲבוֹתֵינוּ אֶרֶץ חֶמְדָּה טוֹבָה וּרְחָבָה וְעַל שֶׁהוֹצֵאתָנוּ יְיָ אֱלֹהֵינוּ מֵאֶרֶץ מִצְרַיִם וּפְדִיתָנוּ מִבֵּית עֲבָדִים וְעַל בְּרִיתְךָ שֶׁחָתַמְתָּ בִּבְשָׂרֵנוּ וְעַל תּוֹרָתְךָ שֶׁלִּמַּדְתָּנוּ וְעַל חֻקֶּיךָ שֶׁהוֹדַעְתָּנוּ וְעַל חַיִּים חֵן וָחֶסֶד שֶׁחוֹנַנְתָּנוּ וְעַל אֲכִילַת מָזוֹן שָׁאַתָּה זָן וּמְפַרְנֵס אוֹתָנוּ תָּמִיד בְּכָל יוֹם וּבְכָל עֵת וּבְכָל שָׁעָה.

וְעַל הַכֹּל יְיָ אֱלֹהֵינוּ אֲנַחְנוּ מוֹדִים לָךְ וּמְבָרְכִים אוֹתָךְ יִתְבָּרֵךְ שִׁמְךָ בְּפִי כָּל חַי תָּמִיד לְעוֹלָם וָעֶד, כַּכָּתוּב: וְאָכַלְתָּ וְשָׂבָעְתָּ וּבֵרַכְתָּ אֶת יְיָ אֱלֹהֶיךָ עַל הָאָרֶץ הַטֹּבָה אֲשֶׁר נָתַן לָךְ. בָּרוּךְ אַתָּה יְיָ, עַל הָאָרֶץ וְעַל הַמָּזוֹן.

רַחֵם יְיָ אֱלֹהֵינוּ עַל יִשְׂרָאֵל עַמֶּךָ וְעַל יְרוּשָׁלַיִם עִירֶךָ וְעַל צִיּוֹן מִשְׁכַּן כְּבוֹדֶךָ וְעַל מַלְכוּת בֵּית דָּוִד מְשִׁיחֶךָ וְעַל הַבַּיִת הַגָּדוֹל וְהַקָּדוֹשׁ שֶׁנִּקְרָא שִׁמְךָ עָלָיו. אֱלֹהֵינוּ אָבִינוּ רוֹעֵנוּ זוֹנֵנוּ פַּרְנְסֵנוּ וְכַלְכְּלֵנוּ וְהַרְוִיחֵנוּ וְהַרְוַח לָנוּ יְיָ אֱלֹהֵינוּ מְהֵרָה מִכָּל צָרוֹתֵינוּ. וְנָא אַל תַּצְרִיכֵנוּ יְיָ אֱלֹהֵינוּ, לֹא לִידֵי מַתְּנַת בָּשָׂר וָדָם וְלֹא לִידֵי הַלְוָאָתָם כִּי אִם לְיָדְךָ הַמְּלֵאָה הַפְּתוּחָה הַקְּדוֹשָׁה וְהָרְחָבָה שֶׁלֹּא נֵבוֹשׁ וְלֹא נִכָּלֵם לְעוֹלָם וָעֶד.

נוֹדֶה **We thank You, Hashem, our God, because You gave** Eretz Yisrael **to our ancestors** as an **inheritance** to be passed down to us. It is a **precious land; a good and wide** open land. We also thank You, **Hashem, our God,** for taking us out of the land of Egypt, for **redeeming us from the house of slaves, for the bris milah You** have commanded us to do, and **that You** have **made in our flesh, for Your Torah, that You taught us, for Your mitzvos that You have made known to us, for the life, graciousness, and kindness that You have kindly given us, and for** the food we **eat, with which You always feed and support us, every day, at all times, and in every hour.**

וְעַל **We thank and bless You, Hashem, our God, for all** the good things You do for us. When Moshiach comes, **Your name will be blessed by the mouths of all living things, always and forever,** because then the world will recognize that You are the only true God. We know that it is a mitzvah to bless Hashem after we eat because **it is written** in the passuk: When **you have eaten and you are satisfied, you should bless Hashem, your God.** You should thank Him **for the good land** of Eretz Yisrael that **He has given you. Blessed are You, Hashem, for the land and for the food** it produces.

רַחֵם **Hashem, our God, have mercy on** B'nei **Yisrael, Your nation. Have** mercy **on Your city, Yerushalayim. Have** mercy **on Tziyon, where Your glory rests. Have** mercy **on the kingship of the House of Dovid. Have** mercy on the royal descendants of Dovid Hamelech, whom You **anointed** to rule over the Jewish people, **and** have mercy **on the great and holy house,** the Beis Hamikdash, **which is called** the "House of Hashem," and is known **by Your name. Our God, our Father, our Shepherd, feed us** with extra food, **provide** clothes and other necessities **for us, support us, and provide us with plenty** of what we need. **Hashem, our God, relieve us speedily from all of our troubles,** both physical and spiritual. **Hashem, our God, please do not** put us in a situation where **we** will **need people's presents or loans** in order to survive. **Instead,** let us get everything we need **from Your full, open, holy, and generous hand,** in order **that we should never be embarrassed or disgraced.**

בְּשַׁבָּת:

On Shabbos, add this paragraph:

רְצֵה וְהַחֲלִיצֵנוּ יְיָ אֱלֹהֵינוּ בְּמִצְוֹתֶיךָ וּבְמִצְוַת יוֹם הַשְּׁבִיעִי הַשַּׁבָּת הַגָּדוֹל וְהַקָּדוֹשׁ הַזֶּה כִּי יוֹם זֶה גָּדוֹל וְקָדוֹשׁ הוּא לְפָנֶיךָ לִשְׁבָּת בּוֹ וְלָנְוּחַ בּוֹ בְּאַהֲבָה כְּמִצְוַת רְצוֹנֶךָ וּבִרְצוֹנְךָ הָנִיחַ לָנוּ יְיָ אֱלֹהֵינוּ שֶׁלֹּא תְהֵא צָרָה וְיָגוֹן וַאֲנָחָה בְּיוֹם מְנוּחָתֵנוּ, וְהַרְאֵנוּ יְיָ אֱלֹהֵינוּ בְּנֶחָמַת צִיּוֹן עִירֶךָ וּבְבִנְיַן יְרוּשָׁלַיִם עִיר קָדְשֶׁךָ כִּי אַתָּה הוּא בַּעַל הַיְשׁוּעוֹת וּבַעַל הַנֶּחָמוֹת.

The leader says the phrases from זָכְרֵנוּ to טוֹבִים
aloud, and the others respond אָמֵן as shown.

אֱלֹהֵינוּ וֵאלֹהֵי אֲבוֹתֵינוּ, יַעֲלֶה וְיָבוֹא וְיַגִּיעַ, וְיֵרָאֶה וְיֵרָצֶה וְיִשָּׁמַע, וְיִפָּקֵד וְיִזָּכֵר זִכְרוֹנֵנוּ וּפִקְדוֹנֵנוּ, וְזִכְרוֹן אֲבוֹתֵינוּ, וְזִכְרוֹן מָשִׁיחַ בֶּן דָּוִד עַבְדֶּךָ, וְזִכְרוֹן יְרוּשָׁלַיִם עִיר קָדְשֶׁךָ, וְזִכְרוֹן כָּל עַמְּךָ בֵּית יִשְׂרָאֵל לְפָנֶיךָ, לִפְלֵיטָה לְטוֹבָה, לְחֵן וּלְחֶסֶד וּלְרַחֲמִים וּלְחַיִּים טוֹבִים וּלְשָׁלוֹם, בְּיוֹם חַג הַמַּצוֹת הַזֶּה, בְּיוֹם טוֹב מִקְרָא קֹדֶשׁ הַזֶּה, זָכְרֵנוּ יְיָ אֱלֹהֵינוּ בּוֹ לְטוֹבָה (אָמֵן), וּפָקְדֵנוּ בוֹ לִבְרָכָה (אָמֵן), וְהוֹשִׁיעֵנוּ בוֹ לְחַיִּים טוֹבִים (אָמֵן), וּבִדְבַר יְשׁוּעָה וְרַחֲמִים, חוּס וְחָנֵּנוּ, וְרַחֵם עָלֵינוּ וְהוֹשִׁיעֵנוּ, כִּי אֵלֶיךָ עֵינֵינוּ, כִּי אֵל מֶלֶךְ חַנּוּן וְרַחוּם אָתָּה.

וּבְנֵה יְרוּשָׁלַיִם עִיר הַקֹּדֶשׁ
בִּמְהֵרָה בְיָמֵינוּ.
בָּרוּךְ אַתָּה יְיָ,
בּוֹנֵה בְרַחֲמָיו יְרוּשָׁלָיִם.
אָמֵן.

Place the cup on the table.

רְצֵה **Hashem, our God,** may You continue to **want to strengthen us** through **Your Mitzvos and through the mitzvah of the seventh day, this great and holy Shabbos. For this day is a great and holy day before You,** a day **in** which **to lovingly stop working and to rest, in accordance with** the **mitzvah that You want** us to do. **Hashem, our God, with Your good will, give us calm;** may we have no hardships on this day, **so that there should be no pain, sadness, or sorrow on the day of our rest. Hashem, our God, show us the comforting of Tziyon, Your city, and the rebuilding of Yerushalayim, Your holy city, because You** are the **Master of salvation and comfort.**

אֱלֹהֵינוּ Hashem, **our God and the God of our fathers, may** the following memories **rise up, come** to You, **reach** You, **be seen, willingly** accepted, **heard, recalled, and remembered** by You: **The memories and recollections of** the good things that **we and our fathers** did for You, **the memory of Moshiach, who is a descendant of Dovid** Hamelech, **Your servant, the memory of Yerushalayim, Your holy city,** which is in ruins, **and the memory of Your entire nation,** B'nei **Yisrael,** who are in galus, should all be remembered **before You.** Remember these things, Hashem, and give us **deliverance** from hardship, **goodness, graciousness, kindness, mercy, good life, and peace, on this** special **day of the Yom Tov of Pesach, on this Yom Tov** that the Torah **calls Holy. Remember us, Hashem, our God, on this** special day **for good** things, **remember us on it for blessing, and help us on this** day to have a **good life.** Hashem, You have promised to help us and have mercy on us. **With this promise of salvation and mercy, have pity** on us, **be kind to us, have mercy on us, and save us, because our eyes** look only **towards You, because You, Hashem, are a kind and merciful King.**

וּבְנֵה Hashem, **rebuild the holy city of Yerushalayim quickly, in our days.**

Blessed are You, Hashem, Who in His mercy rebuilds Yerushalayim.

Amen.

בָּרוּךְ אַתָּה יְיָ, אֱלֹהֵינוּ מֶלֶךְ הָעוֹלָם, הָאֵל, אָבִינוּ מַלְכֵּנוּ, אַדִּירֵנוּ בּוֹרְאֵנוּ גּוֹאֲלֵנוּ יוֹצְרֵנוּ, קְדוֹשֵׁנוּ קְדוֹשׁ יַעֲקֹב, רוֹעֵנוּ רוֹעֵה יִשְׂרָאֵל הַמֶּלֶךְ הַטּוֹב וְהַמֵּטִיב לַכֹּל בְּכָל יוֹם וָיוֹם, הוּא הֵטִיב לָנוּ, הוּא מֵטִיב לָנוּ, הוּא יֵיטִיב לָנוּ, הוּא גְמָלָנוּ הוּא גוֹמְלֵנוּ הוּא יִגְמְלֵנוּ לָעַד, לְחֵן וּלְחֶסֶד וּלְרַחֲמִים, וּלְרֶוַח הַצָּלָה וְהַצְלָחָה, בְּרָכָה וִישׁוּעָה, נֶחָמָה פַּרְנָסָה וְכַלְכָּלָה וְרַחֲמִים וְחַיִּים וְשָׁלוֹם וְכָל טוֹב וּמִכָּל טוּב לְעוֹלָם אַל יְחַסְּרֵנוּ.

הָרַחֲמָן הוּא יִמְלוֹךְ עָלֵינוּ לְעוֹלָם וָעֶד.

הָרַחֲמָן הוּא יִתְבָּרֵךְ בַּשָּׁמַיִם וּבָאָרֶץ.

הָרַחֲמָן הוּא יִשְׁתַּבַּח לְדוֹר דּוֹרִים וְיִתְפָּאַר בָּנוּ לָעַד וּלְנֵצַח נְצָחִים וְיִתְהַדַּר בָּנוּ לָעַד וּלְעוֹלְמֵי עוֹלָמִים.

הָרַחֲמָן הוּא יְפַרְנְסֵנוּ בְּכָבוֹד.

הָרַחֲמָן הוּא יִשְׁבּוֹר עוֹל גָּלוּת מֵעַל צַוָּארֵנוּ וְהוּא יוֹלִיכֵנוּ קוֹמְמִיּוּת לְאַרְצֵנוּ.

הָרַחֲמָן הוּא יִשְׁלַח בְּרָכָה מְרֻבָּה בַּבַּיִת הַזֶּה וְעַל שֻׁלְחָן זֶה שֶׁאָכַלְנוּ עָלָיו.

הָרַחֲמָן הוּא יִשְׁלַח לָנוּ אֶת אֵלִיָּהוּ הַנָּבִיא זָכוּר לַטּוֹב וִיבַשֶּׂר לָנוּ בְּשׂוֹרוֹת טוֹבוֹת יְשׁוּעוֹת וְנֶחָמוֹת.

הָרַחֲמָן הוּא יְבָרֵךְ אֶת אָבִי מוֹרִי בַּעַל הַבַּיִת הַזֶּה וְאֶת אִמִּי מוֹרָתִי בַּעֲלַת הַבַּיִת הַזֶּה אוֹתָם וְאֶת בֵּיתָם וְאֶת זַרְעָם וְאֶת כָּל אֲשֶׁר לָהֶם אוֹתָנוּ וְאֶת כָּל אֲשֶׁר לָנוּ. כְּמוֹ שֶׁבֵּרַךְ אֶת אֲבוֹתֵינוּ אַבְרָהָם יִצְחָק וְיַעֲקֹב בַּכֹּל מִכֹּל כֹּל, כֵּן יְבָרֵךְ אוֹתָנוּ (בְּנֵי בְרִית) כֻּלָּנוּ יַחַד בִּבְרָכָה שְׁלֵמָה וְנֹאמַר אָמֵן.

בָּרוּךְ **Blessed are You, Hashem, our God, King of the world.** You are **the God** of the world, **our Father, our King, our Strength, our Creator, our Redeemer, our Maker, our Holy One** and **the Holy One of Yaakov** and his descendants, B'nei Yisrael. You are **our Shepherd**—the **shepherd** Who guides His flock, B'nei **Yisrael.** You are the **King Who is good and does good things for all, each and every day.** We thank Hashem because **He has done good for us, He does good for us, and He will** continue **to do good for us. He has given us** in the past, **He gives to us** presently, and **He will** continue to **give us,** in the future and **forever,** the following things: **grace, kindness, mercy, relief, rescue** from our troubles, **success, blessings, salvation, comfort, livelihood, support, mercy, life, peace, and all good things.** May Hashem **never let us lack any** of **the good** things in the world.

May Hashem, **the merciful** God, **rule over us forever and ever.**

May Hashem, **the merciful** God, **be blessed in heaven and on earth.**

May Hashem, **the merciful** God, **be praised throughout all generations and be proud of us and be glorified by us forever and ever.**

May Hashem, **the merciful** God, **provide us** with livelihood **in** an **honorable** and dignified way.

May Hashem, **the merciful** God, **break** off the **yoke of galus from our necks.** May He remove the restrictions and hardship of galus from us, **and may He lead us,** standing **upright** and proud, **to** Eretz Yisrael **our land.**

May Hashem, **the merciful** God, **send many blessings** to us **in this house and on this table on which we have eaten.**

May Hashem, **the merciful** God, **send us Eliyahu Hanavi,** who is **remembered for the good** things he did, to **inform us** of the **good news,** that Moshiach is arriving, bringing **comfort and salvation.**

May Hashem, **the merciful** God, **bless my father and teacher, the master of this house, and my mother and teacher,** the **mistress of this house.** Hashem should bless **them, their household, their descendants, and everything that belongs to them,** together with **us and everything that belongs to us. Just as He blessed our forefathers Avraham, Yitzchak, and Yaakov in all things, so too, He should bless all of us together,** in all things, **with a complete blessing. Let us say Amen.**

מִמָּרוֹם יְלַמְּדוּ עָלָיו וְעָלֵינוּ זְכוּת שֶׁתְּהֵא לְמִשְׁמֶרֶת שָׁלוֹם וְנִשָּׂא בְרָכָה מֵאֵת יְיָ וּצְדָקָה מֵאֱלֹהֵי יִשְׁעֵנוּ וְנִמְצָא חֵן וְשֵׂכֶל טוֹב בְּעֵינֵי אֱלֹהִים וְאָדָם.

בְּשַׁבָּת:
On Shabbos add the following line:
הָרַחֲמָן הוּא יַנְחִילֵנוּ לְיוֹם שֶׁכֻּלּוֹ שַׁבָּת וּמְנוּחָה לְחַיֵּי הָעוֹלָמִים.

הָרַחֲמָן הוּא יַנְחִילֵנוּ לְיוֹם שֶׁכֻּלּוֹ טוֹב.

הָרַחֲמָן הוּא יְזַכֵּנוּ לִימוֹת הַמָּשִׁיחַ וּלְחַיֵּי הָעוֹלָם הַבָּא. מִגְדֹּל יְשׁוּעוֹת מַלְכּוֹ וְעֹשֶׂה חֶסֶד לִמְשִׁיחוֹ לְדָוִד וּלְזַרְעוֹ עַד עוֹלָם. עֹשֶׂה שָׁלוֹם בִּמְרוֹמָיו הוּא יַעֲשֶׂה שָׁלוֹם עָלֵינוּ וְעַל כָּל יִשְׂרָאֵל וְאִמְרוּ אָמֵן.

יְראוּ אֶת יְיָ קְדֹשָׁיו, כִּי אֵין מַחְסוֹר לִירֵאָיו. כְּפִירִים רָשׁוּ וְרָעֵבוּ, וְדֹרְשֵׁי יְיָ לֹא יַחְסְרוּ כָל טוֹב. הוֹדוּ לַיְיָ כִּי טוֹב, כִּי לְעוֹלָם חַסְדּוֹ. פּוֹתֵחַ אֶת יָדֶךָ, וּמַשְׂבִּיעַ לְכָל חַי רָצוֹן. בָּרוּךְ הַגֶּבֶר אֲשֶׁר יִבְטַח בַּיְיָ, וְהָיָה יְיָ מִבְטַחוֹ.

וּמְבָרֵךְ עַל הַכּוֹס וְשׁוֹתֶה בַּהֲסִבָּה:
Hold the cup in the same manner as during Kiddush
and say the following brachah for the wine.

בָּרוּךְ אַתָּה יְיָ, אֱלֹהֵינוּ מֶלֶךְ הָעוֹלָם, בּוֹרֵא פְּרִי הַגָּפֶן.

Drink the entire cup (or at least most of it) without interruption while seated and leaning on the left side.

מִמָּרוֹם **May** the angels **ask** Hashem to give **us and** the owner of this home **a** special **privilege from** heaven **above: that there should be long-lasting peace** for all of us and that **we should receive blessing and kindness from Hashem Who saves us. May we find kindness and good understanding in the eyes of Hashem and** all **people;** may Hashem and all people be kind to us and understand us.

הָרַחֲמָן **May** Hashem, **the merciful** God, **give us as an inheritance the day which will be entirely Shabbos and restfulness;** may He give us the geulah through the coming of Moshiach, when there will be true rest and **everlasting life.**

הָרַחֲמָן **May** Hashem, **the merciful** God, **give us as an inheritance the day which is all good;** may He give us the geulah, when there will be only good in the world.

הָרַחֲמָן **May** Hashem, **the merciful** God, **give us the privilege of** living in **the days of Moshiach and** the privilege of **life of Olam Haba.** Hashem is a **tower of salvation** for Dovid Hamelech, **His king.** He does kindness for His **anointed one, Dovid** Hamelech, **and** He will act kindly **to his descendants forever. May Hashem, Who makes peace in His heavens, make peace for us and for all** B'nei **Yisrael, and everyone say Amen.**

יְראוּ **Fear Hashem,** you who are **His holy** people, **because those who fear Him lack nothing.** Even wealthy and powerful people, who are strong like **young lions,** can **become poor and go hungry, but the people who search for Hashem** and rely on Him for their livelihood **will never lack any goodness. Give thanks to Hashem because He is good** to everyone; **because His kindness** lasts **forever.** Hashem, You **open Your hand** and give enough food **to satisfy the desires of every living thing. Blessed is the man who trusts in Hashem, and Hashem will be his security.**

בָּרוּךְ **Blessed are You, Hashem, our God, King of the world, Who creates the fruit of the vine.**

מוֹזְגִין כּוֹס ד' וּפוֹתְחִין הַדֶּלֶת וְאוֹמֵר:

The fourth cup is poured.

- All doors between where the Seder is being conducted and the outside are opened, and the following paragraph is said. Those sent to open the doors say the paragraph at the front door. All others say it while seated.

- On weeknights, it is customary to take lit candles to the front door.

שְׁפֹךְ חֲמָתְךָ אֶל הַגּוֹיִם אֲשֶׁר לֹא יְדָעוּךָ, וְעַל מַמְלָכוֹת אֲשֶׁר בְּשִׁמְךָ לֹא קָרָאוּ. כִּי אָכַל אֶת יַעֲקֹב, וְאֶת נָוֵהוּ הֵשַׁמּוּ. שְׁפָךְ עֲלֵיהֶם זַעְמֶךָ וַחֲרוֹן אַפְּךָ יַשִּׂיגֵם. תִּרְדֹּף בְּאַף וְתַשְׁמִידֵם מִתַּחַת שְׁמֵי יְיָ.

The doors are closed.

SEDER OF THE SEDER

Q Why do we pour the fourth cup right before we say שְׁפֹךְ חֲמָתְךָ?

A There are many answers, including:

- We are saying to Hashem: Now that we have poured the fourth and final cup, we have completed our mitzvah. Now, please do what You promised to do—שְׁפֹךְ חֲמָתְךָ, "pour" your anger and take retribution from those who harmed us.

- The four cups represent the four kingdoms who ruled over us during the four periods of galus: בָּבֶל - Babylonia, פָּרַס - Persia, יָוָן - Greek-Syria, and אֱדוֹם - Rome. The last cup represents the final galus, which we are currently in. We therefore pour it right before שְׁפֹךְ חֲמָתְךָ, which describes what Hashem will do when the final galus ends and the geulah begins.

MINHAGIM

The Rebbeim would fill the Kos Shel Eliyahu themselves.

DID YOU KNOW?

Q Why do we prepare a special cup for Eliyahu Hanavi at the Seder?

A Males must have a bris in order to eat from the Korban Pesach. Eliyahu Hanavi, who visits each bris, is the one who bears testimony that the participants in the Korban Pesach have had a bris.

MINHAGIM

Q Why do we open the door during שְׁפֹךְ חֲמָתְךָ?

A To remind us that the Seder night is "לֵיל שְׁמוּרִים - a guarded night," and we are not afraid of anything. In the zechus of our faith that we will be protected on this night, Moshiach will come, and Hashem will fulfill the requests we ask for in the paragraph of שְׁפֹךְ חֲמָתְךָ.

שְׁפֹךְ Hashem, **pour Your anger onto the nations that do not acknowledge You and onto the kingdoms that do not call** out **Your name, because they have devoured** B'nei **Yisrael and destroyed** their **Beis** Hamikdash. **Pour Your fury against them, and let Your fiery anger overtake them. Chase them with anger, and destroy them from beneath** Your **heavens** — the **heavens of Hashem.**

When those sent to open the doors return, continue with Hallel.

לֹא לָנוּ יְיָ, לֹא לָנוּ, כִּי לְשִׁמְךָ תֵּן כָּבוֹד, עַל חַסְדְּךָ עַל אֲמִתֶּךָ. לָמָּה יֹאמְרוּ הַגּוֹיִם, אַיֵּה נָא אֱלֹהֵיהֶם. וֵאלֹהֵינוּ בַשָּׁמַיִם, כֹּל אֲשֶׁר חָפֵץ עָשָׂה. עֲצַבֵּיהֶם כֶּסֶף וְזָהָב, מַעֲשֵׂה יְדֵי אָדָם. פֶּה לָהֶם וְלֹא יְדַבֵּרוּ, עֵינַיִם לָהֶם וְלֹא יִרְאוּ. אָזְנַיִם לָהֶם וְלֹא יִשְׁמָעוּ, אַף לָהֶם וְלֹא יְרִיחוּן. יְדֵיהֶם וְלֹא יְמִישׁוּן, רַגְלֵיהֶם וְלֹא יְהַלֵּכוּ, לֹא יֶהְגּוּ בִּגְרוֹנָם. כְּמוֹהֶם יִהְיוּ עֹשֵׂיהֶם, כֹּל אֲשֶׁר בֹּטֵחַ בָּהֶם. יִשְׂרָאֵל בְּטַח בַּייָ, עֶזְרָם וּמָגִנָּם הוּא. בֵּית אַהֲרֹן בִּטְחוּ בַייָ, עֶזְרָם וּמָגִנָּם הוּא. יִרְאֵי יְיָ בִּטְחוּ בַייָ, עֶזְרָם וּמָגִנָּם הוּא.

יְיָ זְכָרָנוּ יְבָרֵךְ,

יְבָרֵךְ אֶת בֵּית יִשְׂרָאֵל, יְבָרֵךְ אֶת בֵּית אַהֲרֹן.

יְבָרֵךְ יִרְאֵי יְיָ, הַקְּטַנִּים עִם הַגְּדֹלִים.

יֹסֵף יְיָ עֲלֵיכֶם, עֲלֵיכֶם וְעַל בְּנֵיכֶם.

בְּרוּכִים אַתֶּם לַייָ, עֹשֵׂה שָׁמַיִם וָאָרֶץ.

הַשָּׁמַיִם שָׁמַיִם לַייָ, וְהָאָרֶץ נָתַן לִבְנֵי אָדָם.

לֹא הַמֵּתִים יְהַלְלוּ יָהּ, וְלֹא כָּל יֹרְדֵי דוּמָה.

וַאֲנַחְנוּ נְבָרֵךְ יָהּ, מֵעַתָּה וְעַד עוֹלָם, הַלְלוּיָהּ.

 WORD POWER

Q What does נִרְצָה mean?

A If we have performed the Seder properly until the end, it will be **accepted favorably** by Hashem.

לֹא Not for our sake, Hashem; not because we are deserving should You be kind to us. **Rather, for** the sake of **Your name, give** and shine **Your glory, in order** that the nations should know of **Your kindness and Your truth,** that You always do good to B'nei Yisrael. **Why should the nations** be able to **say** about B'nei Yisrael, **"Where is their God?** Why does He not help them?" **Our God is in heaven;** He is not like the idols of the other nations, which are man-made. **He does whatever He wants,** because He controls everything. The **idols** which the nations of the world worship are made **of silver and gold;** they are **made by human hands. They have a mouth, but cannot speak; they have eyes, but cannot see; they have ears but cannot hear; they have a nose but cannot smell. Their hands cannot touch; their feet cannot walk.** They **cannot** even **make** the smallest **sound with their throats. Those who make** idols and **all those who trust in them will become like them**—unable to speak, see, hear, smell, touch, or walk. B'nei **Yisrael** should **trust in Hashem!** He is their help and their shield to protect them from trouble. Kohanim of the **House of Aharon** should **trust in Hashem!** He is their help and their shield. **Those who fear Hashem** should **trust in Hashem! He is their help and their shield.**

יְיָ **May Hashem,** Who always **remembers us, bless** us. **May He bless** B'nei **Yisrael; may He bless** the Kohanim of **the House of Aharon. May He bless those who fear Hashem, the small,** ordinary people **as well as the great** people. **May Hashem increase** the brachos He puts **upon you; upon you and upon your children. You are blessed** constantly **by Hashem, Who made** the **heavens and** the **earth. The heavens are the heavens of Hashem,** and human beings cannot live in them, but **He gave the earth to human beings** on which to live. **Those who are dead cannot praise Hashem; anyone who goes down into** the **silence** of the grave **cannot** praise Hashem. But **we,** who are still alive on this world, **will bless Hashem from now and forever,** throughout all future generations. **Praise Hashem.**

אָהַבְתִּי, כִּי יִשְׁמַע יְיָ אֶת קוֹלִי תַּחֲנוּנָי. כִּי הִטָּה אָזְנוֹ לִי, וּבְיָמַי אֶקְרָא. אֲפָפוּנִי חֶבְלֵי מָוֶת, וּמְצָרֵי שְׁאוֹל מְצָאוּנִי, צָרָה וְיָגוֹן אֶמְצָא. וּבְשֵׁם יְיָ אֶקְרָא, אָנָּה יְיָ מַלְּטָה נַפְשִׁי. חַנּוּן יְיָ וְצַדִּיק, וֵאלֹהֵינוּ מְרַחֵם. שֹׁמֵר פְּתָאִים יְיָ, דַּלֹּתִי וְלִי יְהוֹשִׁיעַ. שׁוּבִי נַפְשִׁי לִמְנוּחָיְכִי, כִּי יְיָ גָּמַל עָלָיְכִי. כִּי חִלַּצְתָּ נַפְשִׁי מִמָּוֶת, אֶת עֵינִי מִן דִּמְעָה, אֶת רַגְלִי מִדֶּחִי. אֶתְהַלֵּךְ לִפְנֵי יְיָ, בְּאַרְצוֹת הַחַיִּים. הֶאֱמַנְתִּי כִּי אֲדַבֵּר, אֲנִי עָנִיתִי מְאֹד. אֲנִי אָמַרְתִּי בְחָפְזִי, כָּל הָאָדָם כֹּזֵב.

מָה אָשִׁיב לַיְיָ, כָּל תַּגְמוּלוֹהִי עָלָי. כּוֹס יְשׁוּעוֹת אֶשָּׂא, וּבְשֵׁם יְיָ אֶקְרָא. נְדָרַי לַיְיָ אֲשַׁלֵּם, נֶגְדָה נָּא לְכָל עַמּוֹ. יָקָר בְּעֵינֵי יְיָ, הַמָּוְתָה לַחֲסִידָיו. אָנָּה יְיָ כִּי אֲנִי עַבְדֶּךָ, אֲנִי עַבְדְּךָ בֶּן אֲמָתֶךָ, פִּתַּחְתָּ לְמוֹסֵרָי. לְךָ אֶזְבַּח זֶבַח תּוֹדָה, וּבְשֵׁם יְיָ אֶקְרָא. נְדָרַי לַיְיָ אֲשַׁלֵּם, נֶגְדָה נָּא לְכָל עַמּוֹ. בְּחַצְרוֹת בֵּית יְיָ, בְּתוֹכֵכִי יְרוּשָׁלָיִם, הַלְלוּיָהּ.

הַלְלוּ אֶת יְיָ כָּל גּוֹיִם,
שַׁבְּחוּהוּ כָּל הָאֻמִּים.

כִּי גָבַר עָלֵינוּ חַסְדּוֹ,
וֶאֱמֶת יְיָ לְעוֹלָם,
הַלְלוּיָהּ.

אָהַבְתִּי Dovid Hamelech said: **I love** Hashem **because Hashem** always **listens to my voice** and **my tefillos. He turns His ear towards me** and listens to me **on the days** that **I call** to Him. When Shaul almost killed me, **a** sudden **feeling of death surrounded me, and the tight space of the grave came upon me.** At that time, **I found** myself filled with **pain and sadness.** So **I called out with the name of Hashem** and said, **"Hashem, I beg You to save my soul!"** I called out to **Hashem** because He **is kind and righteous; our God is merciful. Hashem watches over simple** people, who do not know how to stay away from bad things, and **He saves them. When I was** in **my low,** sad situation, **He saved me. My soul, return** peacefully **to** Hashem, because there you will find **your rest. Hashem** has always **given you kindness.** Hashem, **You have saved my soul from death.** You have saved **my eyes from tears, and** You saved **my feet from falling** when I was running from my enemies. **I will** now **walk before Hashem in the lands of** Eretz Yisrael, among **the** people **living** in peace. Hashem, **I had faith** that You would save me, even **when I said, "I am in great suffering."** Even when people said that I would never be king, I had faith. **As I hurried** and ran away from Shaul **I said, "All the people** who are saying that I will never be king **are** being **dishonest."**

מָה **How can I repay Hashem for all of His** acts of **kindness which He** has done **for me? I will raise a cup** of wine and tell B'nei Yisrael about how You **saved me, and I will call in the name of Hashem. I will pay** and keep **my promises** to Hashem, which I committed to fulfill if He saved me from danger, **now, while in the presence of all of** B'nei Yisrael, **His people. It is painful in the eyes of Hashem** to see **the death of His devoted people,** and that is why He performs miracles to save them. **I thank** You, **Hashem,** for the fact **that I am Your** humble **servant. I am Your servant;** I am the humble **son of** my mother, **Your maidservant.** Because I have been humble, **You have loosened** the knots that **tied me,** and I have been saved. **I will shecht** a korban **to You, an offering of thanks; and I will call in the name of Hashem. I will pay** and keep **my promises** to **Hashem,** which I committed to fulfill if He saved me from danger. I will do this **now, while in the presence of all of** B'nei Yisrael, **His people, in the courtyards of the House of Hashem**—the Beis Hamikdash, which **is in the midst of** Yerushalayim. Praise Hashem.

הַלְלוּ **When Moshiach comes, all the nations** will **praise Hashem;** all the **people** will **glorify Him.**

They will praise Him **because His kindness was mighty over us. The truth of Hashem is everlasting;** He is trusted to keep His promises forever. **Praise Hashem.**

The four pessukim in grey type are said aloud by the leader. After each passuk, the others answer "...הוֹדוּ לַיְיָ," and then say the next passuk quietly as shown. The leader also says "...הוֹדוּ לַיְיָ" after each of the last three pessukim.

Leader – הוֹדוּ לַיְיָ כִּי טוֹב, כִּי לְעוֹלָם חַסְדּוֹ.

Others – הוֹדוּ לַיְיָ כִּי טוֹב, כִּי לְעוֹלָם חַסְדּוֹ.
יֹאמַר נָא יִשְׂרָאֵל, כִּי לְעוֹלָם חַסְדּוֹ.

Leader – יֹאמַר נָא יִשְׂרָאֵל, כִּי לְעוֹלָם חַסְדּוֹ.

Others – הוֹדוּ לַיְיָ כִּי טוֹב, כִּי לְעוֹלָם חַסְדּוֹ.
יֹאמְרוּ נָא בֵית אַהֲרֹן, כִּי לְעוֹלָם חַסְדּוֹ.

Leader – יֹאמְרוּ נָא בֵית אַהֲרֹן, כִּי לְעוֹלָם חַסְדּוֹ.

Others – הוֹדוּ לַיְיָ כִּי טוֹב, כִּי לְעוֹלָם חַסְדּוֹ.
יֹאמְרוּ נָא יִרְאֵי יְיָ, כִּי לְעוֹלָם חַסְדּוֹ.

Leader – יֹאמְרוּ נָא יִרְאֵי יְיָ, כִּי לְעוֹלָם חַסְדּוֹ.

Others – הוֹדוּ לַיְיָ כִּי טוֹב, כִּי לְעוֹלָם חַסְדּוֹ.

מִן הַמֵּצַר קָרָאתִי יָּה, עָנָנִי בַמֶּרְחָב יָּה. יְיָ לִי לֹא אִירָא, מַה יַּעֲשֶׂה לִי אָדָם. יְיָ לִי בְּעֹזְרָי, וַאֲנִי אֶרְאֶה בְשֹׂנְאָי. טוֹב לַחֲסוֹת בַּיְיָ, מִבְּטֹחַ בָּאָדָם. טוֹב לַחֲסוֹת בַּיְיָ, מִבְּטֹחַ בִּנְדִיבִים. כָּל גּוֹיִם סְבָבוּנִי, בְּשֵׁם יְיָ כִּי אֲמִילַם. סַבּוּנִי גַם סְבָבוּנִי, בְּשֵׁם יְיָ כִּי אֲמִילַם. סַבּוּנִי כִדְבֹרִים דֹעֲכוּ כְּאֵשׁ קוֹצִים, בְּשֵׁם יְיָ כִּי אֲמִילַם. דָּחֹה דְחִיתַנִי לִנְפֹּל, וַיְיָ עֲזָרָנִי. עָזִּי וְזִמְרָת יָהּ, וַיְהִי לִי לִישׁוּעָה. קוֹל רִנָּה וִישׁוּעָה בְּאָהֳלֵי צַדִּיקִים, יְמִין יְיָ עֹשָׂה חָיִל. יְמִין יְיָ רוֹמֵמָה, יְמִין יְיָ עֹשָׂה חָיִל. לֹא אָמוּת כִּי אֶחְיֶה, וַאֲסַפֵּר מַעֲשֵׂי יָהּ. יַסֹּר יִסְּרַנִי יָּהּ, וְלַמָּוֶת לֹא נְתָנָנִי. פִּתְחוּ לִי שַׁעֲרֵי צֶדֶק, אָבֹא בָם אוֹדֶה יָהּ. זֶה הַשַּׁעַר לַיְיָ, צַדִּיקִים יָבֹאוּ בוֹ.

הוֹדוּ Give **praise to Hashem because** He is **good; because His kindness lasts forever.**

יֹאמַר All of B'nei **Yisrael should say that His kindness lasts forever.**

יֹאמְרוּ The Kohanim of the **House of Aharon should say that His kindness lasts forever.**

יֹאמְרוּ **Those who fear Hashem should say that His kindness lasts forever.**

מִן **From the tight** situation that I was in, **I called** out to **Hashem** for His help. **Hashem answered me** and put me in **a wide open,** peaceful **place. Hashem is with me** and **I will not be afraid of** anyone. **What can** any **person do to me** if I have Hashem's help? When **Hashem is with me, among my helpers, I will see** the downfall of **my enemies. It is better to rely on Hashem** for help **than to trust in any person. It is better to rely on Hashem** for help **than to trust in important,** powerful **people. All the nations surrounded me** to fight me, but I still trusted in You. **In the name of Hashem I will cut them down** and defeat them. **They surrounded me and circled me,** but I still trusted that **in the name of Hashem I will cut them down. They surrounded me like bees** surrounding a jar of honey, but **they will retreat** and fall **like** small **twigs** burning in **a fire. In the name of Hashem I will cut them down. They** constantly **pushed me to** make me **fall, but Hashem helped me,** and I was saved. **Hashem is my strength and song, and He has been a salvation for me. The sound of rejoicing and salvation will be heard in the tents of the tzaddikim** who were saved by Hashem. They will say, **"The right hand of Hashem acts with** great **strength. The right hand of Hashem is raised high; the right hand of Hashem acts with** great **strength." I will not die.** Rather, **I will** continue to **live, and I will tell the** great things **Hashem has done. Hashem** indeed **punished me** for my aveiros, but **He did not to put me to death.** Hashem, **open up the gates of** the Beis Hamikdash—the place of **righteousness**— and **I will enter** through **them and praise** You, Hashem. **This is the gate of Hashem; the tzaddikim will come through it.**

אוֹדְךָ כִּי עֲנִיתָנִי, וַתְּהִי לִי לִישׁוּעָה. אוֹדְךָ כִּי עֲנִיתָנִי, וַתְּהִי לִי לִישׁוּעָה. אֶבֶן מָאֲסוּ הַבּוֹנִים, הָיְתָה לְרֹאשׁ פִּנָּה. אֶבֶן מָאֲסוּ הַבּוֹנִים, הָיְתָה לְרֹאשׁ פִּנָּה. מֵאֵת יְיָ הָיְתָה זֹּאת, הִיא נִפְלָאת בְּעֵינֵינוּ. מֵאֵת יְיָ הָיְתָה זֹּאת, הִיא נִפְלָאת בְּעֵינֵינוּ. זֶה הַיּוֹם עָשָׂה יְיָ, נָגִילָה וְנִשְׂמְחָה בוֹ. זֶה הַיּוֹם עָשָׂה יְיָ, נָגִילָה וְנִשְׂמְחָה בוֹ.

Each of the following four lines is said aloud by
the leader, followed by everyone else.

אָנָּא יְיָ הוֹשִׁיעָה נָּא.

אָנָּא יְיָ הוֹשִׁיעָה נָּא.

אָנָּא יְיָ הַצְלִיחָה נָא.

אָנָּא יְיָ הַצְלִיחָה נָא.

בָּרוּךְ הַבָּא בְּשֵׁם יְיָ, בֵּרַכְנוּכֶם מִבֵּית יְיָ. בָּרוּךְ הַבָּא בְּשֵׁם יְיָ, בֵּרַכְנוּכֶם מִבֵּית יְיָ. אֵל יְיָ וַיָּאֶר לָנוּ, אִסְרוּ חַג בַּעֲבֹתִים, עַד קַרְנוֹת הַמִּזְבֵּחַ. אֵל יְיָ וַיָּאֶר לָנוּ, אִסְרוּ חַג בַּעֲבֹתִים, עַד קַרְנוֹת הַמִּזְבֵּחַ.

אֵלִי אַתָּה וְאוֹדֶךָּ, אֱלֹהַי אֲרוֹמְמֶךָּ.

אֵלִי אַתָּה וְאוֹדֶךָּ, אֱלֹהַי אֲרוֹמְמֶךָּ.

הוֹדוּ לַיְיָ כִּי טוֹב, כִּי לְעוֹלָם חַסְדּוֹ.

הוֹדוּ לַיְיָ כִּי טוֹב, כִּי לְעוֹלָם חַסְדּוֹ.

יְהַלְלוּךָ יְיָ אֱלֹהֵינוּ (עַל) כָּל מַעֲשֶׂיךָ, וַחֲסִידֶיךָ צַדִּיקִים עוֹשֵׂי רְצוֹנֶךָ, וְכָל עַמְּךָ בֵּית יִשְׂרָאֵל, בְּרִנָּה יוֹדוּ וִיבָרְכוּ, וִישַׁבְּחוּ וִיפָאֲרוּ, וִירוֹמְמוּ וְיַעֲרִיצוּ, וְיַקְדִּישׁוּ וְיַמְלִיכוּ אֶת שִׁמְךָ מַלְכֵּנוּ. כִּי לְךָ טוֹב לְהוֹדוֹת, וּלְשִׁמְךָ נָאֶה לְזַמֵּר, כִּי מֵעוֹלָם וְעַד עוֹלָם אַתָּה אֵל.

Hashem, **I thank You because You have answered me** when I called out for You, **and You have been a salvation to me. I thank You because You have answered me, and You have been a salvation to me. I** was like **a stone that the builders did not like,** and did not want to use to build anything, but with Your help I **became as the chief cornerstone,** which is the most important brick in a building. **I** was like **a stone that the builders did not like,** but with Your help I **became** as **the chief cornerstone. This came about from Hashem. It is wondrous in our eyes;** we are amazed that Hashem has done all of these great things for us. **This came about from Hashem. It is wondrous in our eyes. This is the day that Hashem has created, let us be joyful and happy with it. This is the day that Hashem has created, let us be joyful and happy with it.**

אָנָּא **We beg You, Hashem,** please **save us now!**
אָנָּא **We beg You, Hashem,** please **save us now!**

אָנָּא **We beg You, Hashem,** please **grant us success now!**
אָנָּא **We beg You, Hashem,** please **grant us success now!**

בָּרוּךְ The Kohanim would say to people who came to bring bikkurim and korbanos: **Blessed is the** person **who comes** to the Beis Hamikdash **in the name of Hashem. We bless you from the House of Hashem,** the Beis Hamikdash. **Blessed is the** person **who comes in the name of Hashem. We bless you from the House of Hashem. Hashem is a** kind **God, and He has given us light** during times of darkness. We bring korbanos to thank Him for this. **Tie up the Yom Tov korban with cords until** you bring it to **the corners of the Mizbei'ach. Hashem is a** kind **God, and He has given us light. Tie up the Yom Tov korban with cords until** you bring it to **the corners of the Mizbei'ach.**

Those who came up would respond: **You are my God, and I will praise You** for all the great things You have done for B'nei Yisrael. **I will raise You high** by praising You, because You are **my God. You are my God, and I will praise You. I will raise You high, my God. Give praise to Hashem because** He is **good; because His kindness lasts forever. Give** praise **to Hashem because** He is **good; because His kindness lasts forever.**

יְהַלְלוּךְ **Hashem, our God, everything** which **You have created will praise You. Your devoted** people, **the tzaddikim who do Your will, and all of** B'nei **Yisrael, Your nation, will thank Your name and bless** it with **a joyous song.** Hashem, **our King, they will praise Your name, make** it **beautiful, raise** it **high, worship** it, **make** it **holy, and declare** You as **King.** We will do this **because it is good to praise You, and it is fitting** for us **to sing to Your name, because You are Hashem,** Who rules from **the** highest **world to the lowest world.**

There are twenty-six pessukim in this perek, corresponding to the gematriya (numerical value) of Hashem's Name י-ה-ו-ה. When saying the first ten pessukim, one should have in mind (but not say) the י of the Name; for the next five pessukim, have in mind the letter ה of the Name; for the next six pessukim, the letter ו of the Name; and for the last five pessukim, the second letter ה of the Name.

הוֹדוּ לַיָי כִּי טוֹב,   כִּי לְעוֹלָם חַסְדּוֹ.

הוֹדוּ לֵאלֹהֵי הָאֱלֹהִים,   כִּי לְעוֹלָם חַסְדּוֹ.

הוֹדוּ לַאֲדֹנֵי הָאֲדֹנִים,   כִּי לְעוֹלָם חַסְדּוֹ.

לְעֹשֵׂה נִפְלָאוֹת גְּדֹלוֹת לְבַדּוֹ,   כִּי לְעוֹלָם חַסְדּוֹ.

לְעֹשֵׂה הַשָּׁמַיִם בִּתְבוּנָה,   כִּי לְעוֹלָם חַסְדּוֹ.

לְרוֹקַע הָאָרֶץ עַל הַמָּיִם,   כִּי לְעוֹלָם חַסְדּוֹ.

לְעֹשֵׂה אוֹרִים גְּדֹלִים,   כִּי לְעוֹלָם חַסְדּוֹ.

אֶת הַשֶּׁמֶשׁ לְמֶמְשֶׁלֶת בַּיּוֹם,   כִּי לְעוֹלָם חַסְדּוֹ.

אֶת הַיָּרֵחַ וְכוֹכָבִים לְמֶמְשְׁלוֹת בַּלָּיְלָה, כִּי לְעוֹלָם חַסְדּוֹ.

לְמַכֵּה מִצְרַיִם בִּבְכוֹרֵיהֶם, (י)   כִּי לְעוֹלָם חַסְדּוֹ.

וַיּוֹצֵא יִשְׂרָאֵל מִתּוֹכָם,   כִּי לְעוֹלָם חַסְדּוֹ.

בְּיָד חֲזָקָה וּבִזְרוֹעַ נְטוּיָה,   כִּי לְעוֹלָם חַסְדּוֹ.

DID YOU KNOW?

This perek of Tehillim is called Hallel Hagadol — the Great Praise. There are many reasons for this name, including:

- It describes how Hashem gives food to all living creatures, which is a great thing.
- Its 26 pessukim correspond to Hashem's Great Name י-ה-ו-ה.
- Its 26 pessukim correspond to the 26 generations before the Torah was given. Because the world only exists for B'nei Yisrael to learn and fulfill the Torah, in those 26 generations when the Torah was not yet given, Hashem sustained the world from His great kindness.
- This is the praise that the great angels sing to Hashem.

הוֹדוּ Give **praise to Hashem because** He is **good;** because His kindness lasts forever.

Give **praise to the God of the malachim,** because His kindness lasts forever.

Give **praise to the Master of the heavenly creations**—the sun, moon, and stars who serve the world according to His wishes—**because His kindness lasts forever.**

Give praise **to** Hashem, **Who performs great wonders** and miracles **alone,** without any help from anything else, **because His kindness lasts forever.**

Give praise **to** Hashem, **Who creates the heavens with** great **understanding,** making sure they provide the earth with its needs, **because His kindness lasts forever.**

Give praise **to** Hashem, **Who spreads the earth out over the water** and makes dry land, **because His kindness lasts forever.**

Give praise **to** Hashem, **Who made the great** things that give **light**—the sun, moon, and stars— **because His kindness lasts forever.**

Give praise to Hashem, Who creates **the sun to rule** and shine **during the day, because His kindness lasts forever.**

Give praise to Hashem, Who creates **the moon and stars to rule at night, because His kindness lasts forever.**

Give praise **to** Hashem, **Who struck** and killed many **Egyptians** through **their** own **firstborns** by causing a civil war, **because His kindness lasts forever.**

Give praise to Hashem, Who **took** B'nei **Yisrael out from among the** Egyptians, **because His kindness lasts forever.**

Give praise to Hashem, Who took us out from Egypt **with a strong hand and an outstretched arm, because His kindness lasts forever.**

לְגֹזֵר יַם סוּף לִגְזָרִים,   כִּי לְעוֹלָם חַסְדּוֹ.

וְהֶעֱבִיר יִשְׂרָאֵל בְּתוֹכוֹ,   כִּי לְעוֹלָם חַסְדּוֹ.

וְנִעֵר פַּרְעֹה וְחֵילוֹ בְיַם סוּף,   (ה)   כִּי לְעוֹלָם חַסְדּוֹ.

לְמוֹלִיךְ עַמּוֹ בַּמִּדְבָּר,   כִּי לְעוֹלָם חַסְדּוֹ.

לְמַכֵּה מְלָכִים גְּדֹלִים,   כִּי לְעוֹלָם חַסְדּוֹ.

וַיַּהֲרֹג מְלָכִים אַדִּירִים,   כִּי לְעוֹלָם חַסְדּוֹ.

לְסִיחוֹן מֶלֶךְ הָאֱמֹרִי,   כִּי לְעוֹלָם חַסְדּוֹ.

וּלְעוֹג מֶלֶךְ הַבָּשָׁן,   כִּי לְעוֹלָם חַסְדּוֹ.

וְנָתַן אַרְצָם לְנַחֲלָה,   (ו)   כִּי לְעוֹלָם חַסְדּוֹ.

נַחֲלָה לְיִשְׂרָאֵל עַבְדּוֹ,   כִּי לְעוֹלָם חַסְדּוֹ.

שֶׁבְּשִׁפְלֵנוּ זָכַר לָנוּ,   כִּי לְעוֹלָם חַסְדּוֹ.

וַיִּפְרְקֵנוּ מִצָּרֵינוּ,   כִּי לְעוֹלָם חַסְדּוֹ.

נוֹתֵן לֶחֶם לְכָל בָּשָׂר,   כִּי לְעוֹלָם חַסְדּוֹ.

הוֹדוּ לְאֵל הַשָּׁמָיִם,   (ה)   כִּי לְעוֹלָם חַסְדּוֹ.

Give praise **to** Hashem, **Who split the Yam Suf into** twelve **sections,** making a path for each shevet, **because His kindness lasts forever.**

Give praise to Hashem, Who **brought** B'nei **Yisrael across** the Yam Suf, **because His kindness lasts forever.**

Give praise to Hashem, Who **threw Paraoh and his** entire **army into the Yam Suf, because His kindness lasts forever.**

Give praise **to** Hashem, **Who led His nation through the desert** with the clouds of glory and pillar of fire, **because His kindness lasts forever.**

Give praise **to** Hashem, **Who struck down** and defeated **great kings, because His kindness lasts forever.**

Give praise to Hashem, Who **killed mighty kings** so that B'nei Yisrael could conquer Eretz Yisrael, **because His kindness lasts forever.**

Give praise to Hashem, Who killed **Sichon,** the **king of the Amorites, because His kindness lasts forever.**

Give praise to Hashem, Who killed **Og, the king of Bashan, because His kindness lasts forever.**

Give praise to Hashem, Who **gave their land,** Eretz Yisrael, **as an inheritance** for B'nei Yisrael, **because His kindness lasts forever.**

Give praise to Hashem, Who gave Eretz Yisrael as **an inheritance to** the children of **Yisrael** (Yaakov) **His servant, because His kindness lasts forever.**

Give praise to Hashem, Who **remembered us** when **our** spirits were **low** in Egypt, **because His kindness lasts forever.**

Give praise to Hashem, Who **freed us from the people who made us suffer, because His kindness lasts forever.**

Give praise to Hashem, Who **gives food to all** creatures of **flesh,** not just humans, **because His kindness lasts forever.**

Give **praise to the God of the heavens,** Who provides rain for food to grow, **because His kindness lasts forever.**

נִשְׁמַת כָּל חַי תְּבָרֵךְ אֶת שִׁמְךָ יְיָ אֱלֹהֵינוּ, וְרוּחַ כָּל בָּשָׂר תְּפָאֵר וּתְרוֹמֵם זִכְרְךָ מַלְכֵּנוּ תָּמִיד, מִן הָעוֹלָם וְעַד הָעוֹלָם אַתָּה אֵל, וּמִבַּלְעָדֶיךָ אֵין לָנוּ מֶלֶךְ גּוֹאֵל וּמוֹשִׁיעַ, פּוֹדֶה וּמַצִּיל וּמְפַרְנֵס וְעוֹנֶה וּמְרַחֵם בְּכָל עֵת צָרָה וְצוּקָה, אֵין לָנוּ מֶלֶךְ אֶלָּא אַתָּה, אֱלֹהֵי הָרִאשׁוֹנִים וְהָאַחֲרוֹנִים. אֱלוֹהַּ כָּל בְּרִיּוֹת, אֲדוֹן כָּל תּוֹלָדוֹת, הַמְהֻלָּל בְּרוֹב הַתִּשְׁבָּחוֹת, הַמְנַהֵג עוֹלָמוֹ בְּחֶסֶד וּבְרִיּוֹתָיו בְּרַחֲמִים. וַיְיָ הִנֵּה לֹא יָנוּם וְלֹא יִישָׁן, הַמְּעוֹרֵר יְשֵׁנִים, וְהַמֵּקִיץ נִרְדָּמִים, וְהַמֵּשִׂיחַ אִלְּמִים, וְהַמַּתִּיר אֲסוּרִים, וְהַסּוֹמֵךְ נוֹפְלִים, וְהַזּוֹקֵף כְּפוּפִים, לְךָ לְבַדְּךָ אֲנַחְנוּ מוֹדִים.

אִלּוּ פִינוּ מָלֵא שִׁירָה כַּיָּם, וּלְשׁוֹנֵנוּ רִנָּה כַּהֲמוֹן גַּלָּיו, וְשִׂפְתוֹתֵינוּ שֶׁבַח כְּמֶרְחֲבֵי רָקִיעַ, וְעֵינֵינוּ מְאִירוֹת כַּשֶּׁמֶשׁ וְכַיָּרֵחַ, וְיָדֵינוּ פְרוּשׂוֹת כְּנִשְׁרֵי שָׁמָיִם, וְרַגְלֵינוּ קַלּוֹת כָּאַיָּלוֹת, אֵין אֲנוּ מַסְפִּיקִים לְהוֹדוֹת לְךָ יְיָ אֱלֹהֵינוּ וֵאלֹהֵי אֲבוֹתֵינוּ, וּלְבָרֵךְ אֶת שְׁמֶךָ עַל אַחַת מֵאֶלֶף אַלְפֵי אֲלָפִים, וְרִבֵּי רְבָבוֹת פְּעָמִים, הַטּוֹבוֹת נִסִּים וְנִפְלָאוֹת שֶׁעָשִׂיתָ עִמָּנוּ וְעִם אֲבוֹתֵינוּ מִלְּפָנִים. מִמִּצְרַיִם גְּאַלְתָּנוּ, יְיָ אֱלֹהֵינוּ, מִבֵּית עֲבָדִים פְּדִיתָנוּ, בְּרָעָב זַנְתָּנוּ, וּבְשָׂבָע כִּלְכַּלְתָּנוּ, מֵחֶרֶב הִצַּלְתָּנוּ, וּמִדֶּבֶר מִלַּטְתָּנוּ, וּמֵחֳלָיִם רָעִים וְנֶאֱמָנִים דִּלִּיתָנוּ. עַד הֵנָּה עֲזָרוּנוּ רַחֲמֶיךָ וְלֹא עֲזָבוּנוּ חֲסָדֶיךָ, וְאַל תִּטְּשֵׁנוּ יְיָ אֱלֹהֵינוּ, לָנֶצַח.

עַל כֵּן, אֵבָרִים שֶׁפִּלַּגְתָּ בָּנוּ, וְרוּחַ וּנְשָׁמָה שֶׁנָּפַחְתָּ בְּאַפֵּינוּ, וְלָשׁוֹן אֲשֶׁר שַׂמְתָּ בְּפִינוּ. הֵן הֵם: יוֹדוּ וִיבָרְכוּ

נִשְׁמַת Hashem, our God—the neshamah of every living thing will bless Your name. Hashem our King, the spirit of all flesh will always glorify and raise Your remembrance high. From this world to the world of Olam Haba, You are the God Who rules with strength. Besides You, Hashem, we have no other king, redeemer, and rescuer who redeems us, rescues us, provides for us, answers our tefillos, and is merciful in all times of trouble and difficulty. We have no King besides You, God of all generations—from the first generations of the world to the last. Hashem is the God of all creations and the Master of everything that happens. He is praised with many types of praises. He guides His world with kindness and His creations with mercy. Indeed, Hashem never stops watching over the world; He is like a guard who does not sleep and does not slumber. Hashem wakes up those who sleep; He even awakens those who sleep deeply. He causes mute people to talk, frees those who are imprisoned, supports those who fall, and straightens those whose backs are bent. To You alone, Hashem, we must give thanks for doing these things.

Even if our mouths were filled with songs of praise for You as the sea is filled with water, and our tongues were filled with song as the roar of the waves of the sea, and our lips filled with praise as wide as the sky, and our eyes shined as bright as the sun and the moon, and our hands were spread out with joy and praise as wings of eagles in the sky, and our feet were as swift to do Your mitzvos as a deer—even if we had all of these qualities, we would still not be able to thank You enough, Hashem, our God, and the God of our fathers, and we would still not be able to bless Your name enough for even one of the countless favors, miracles, and wonders that You have done for us and for our ancestors before us. Hashem, our God, You redeemed us from Egypt; You released us from the house of slaves. You fed us during times of famine and You supported us during times of plenty. You saved us from the sword of our enemies and let us escape from plagues. You kept us away from bad, long-lasting sicknesses. Until now, Your mercy has helped us and Your kindness has not left us. Hashem, our God, You will never abandon us. Therefore, we will thank You for all the great things You have done for us.

The body parts that You have arranged in us, the spirit and the neshamah that You have blown into our nostrils, and the tongues that You have put into our mouths—they will all thank, bless,

וְיִשְׁתַּבְּחוּ וִיפָאֲרוּ, וִירוֹמְמוּ וְיַעֲרִיצוּ, וְיַקְדִּישׁוּ וְיַמְלִיכוּ אֶת שִׁמְךָ מַלְכֵּנוּ.

כִּי כָל פֶּה לְךָ יוֹדֶה, וְכָל לָשׁוֹן לְךָ תִשָּׁבַע, וְכָל עַיִן לְךָ תְצַפֶּה, וְכָל בֶּרֶךְ לְךָ תִכְרַע, וְכָל קוֹמָה לְפָנֶיךָ תִשְׁתַּחֲוֶה, וְכָל הַלְּבָבוֹת יִירָאוּךָ, וְכָל קֶרֶב וּכְלָיוֹת יְזַמְּרוּ לִשְׁמֶךָ, כַּדָּבָר שֶׁכָּתוּב: כָּל עַצְמוֹתַי תֹּאמַרְנָה, יְיָ, מִי כָמוֹךָ, מַצִּיל עָנִי מֵחָזָק מִמֶּנּוּ, וְעָנִי וְאֶבְיוֹן מִגֹּזְלוֹ. מִי יִדְמֶה לָּךְ, וּמִי יִשְׁוֶה לָּךְ, וּמִי יַעֲרָךְ לָךְ, הָאֵל **הַגָּדוֹל, הַגִּבּוֹר וְהַנּוֹרָא**, אֵל עֶלְיוֹן, קֹנֵה שָׁמַיִם וָאָרֶץ. נְהַלֶּלְךָ וּנְשַׁבֵּחֲךָ וּנְפָאֶרְךָ וּנְבָרֵךְ אֶת שֵׁם קָדְשֶׁךָ כָּאמוּר: לְדָוִד, בָּרְכִי נַפְשִׁי אֶת יְיָ, וְכָל קְרָבַי אֶת שֵׁם קָדְשׁוֹ.

הָאֵל בְּתַעֲצֻמוֹת עֻזֶּךָ הַגָּדוֹל בִּכְבוֹד שְׁמֶךָ הַגִּבּוֹר לָנֶצַח, וְהַנּוֹרָא בְּנוֹרְאוֹתֶיךָ הַמֶּלֶךְ הַיּוֹשֵׁב עַל כִּסֵּא רָם וְנִשָּׂא.

שׁוֹכֵן עַד, מָרוֹם וְקָדוֹשׁ שְׁמוֹ, וְכָתוּב: רַנְּנוּ צַדִּיקִים בַּיְיָ, לַיְשָׁרִים נָאוָה תְהִלָּה. בְּפִי יְשָׁרִים תִּתְרוֹמָם, וּבְשִׂפְתֵי צַדִּיקִים תִּתְבָּרֵךְ, וּבִלְשׁוֹן חֲסִידִים תִּתְקַדָּשׁ, וּבְקֶרֶב קְדוֹשִׁים תִּתְהַלָּל.

וּבְמַקְהֲלוֹת רִבְבוֹת עַמְּךָ בֵּית יִשְׂרָאֵל, בְּרִנָּה יִתְפָּאֵר שִׁמְךָ מַלְכֵּנוּ בְּכָל דּוֹר וָדוֹר. שֶׁכֵּן חוֹבַת כָּל הַיְצוּרִים, לְפָנֶיךָ יְיָ אֱלֹהֵינוּ וֵאלֹהֵי אֲבוֹתֵינוּ: לְהוֹדוֹת, לְהַלֵּל, לְשַׁבֵּחַ, לְפָאֵר, לְרוֹמֵם, לְהַדֵּר, לְבָרֵךְ, לְעַלֵּה וּלְקַלֵּס, עַל כָּל דִּבְרֵי שִׁירוֹת וְתִשְׁבְּחוֹת דָּוִד בֶּן יִשַׁי עַבְדְּךָ מְשִׁיחֶךָ.

praise, make beautiful, raise high, worship, make holy, and declare as king—Your name, Hashem, our King.

Hashem, **every mouth will thank You. Every tongue will make an oath in Your** name only. **Every eye will look to You** for help. **Every knee will bend to You. All who stand straight will bow before You. Every** person's **heart will fear You. Every** person's **innermost feelings and thoughts will sing** praises **to Your name.** All of this will happen, **as it is written** in Tehillim: **All of my bones** and my entire body **will say, "Hashem, who is like You?** You **save a poor person from someone who is stronger than him, and** You save **a poor person and a needy person from someone who** wants to **rob him." Hashem, who is similar to You?** Who is **equal to You?** Who is **comparable to You, the mighty, great, powerful, awesome,** and most **high God,** the **creator of heaven and earth? We will laud, praise, and glorify You, and we will bless Your holy name.** As it is said by Dovid Hamelech in Tehillim: **My soul** should **bless Hashem and my entire being should** bless **His holy name.**

הָאֵל You are called **the mighty** God **due to the strength of Your power.** You are called **the great** God **due to the honor of Your name.** You are called **the powerful** God **forever, and** You are called **the awesome** God **due to Your awe-inspiring deeds.**

Hashem, You are **the King Who sits on a high and raised throne.**

שׁוֹכֵן **The Name of** Hashem, **Who dwells forever, is raised high and holy. It is written** in Tehillim: **Tzaddikim** should **sing** praises **to Hashem.** It is **fitting for** those who go in the **straight,** righteous ways of Hashem to **praise** Him. Hashem, **You will be raised high by** the praises which come from **the mouths of** those who go in Your **straight** and righteous ways. **You will be blessed by the lips of tzaddikim. You will be made holy by the tongue of righteous people, and You will be praised among holy** people.

וּבְמַקְהֲלוֹת **In the gatherings of the many people of Your nation, the House of Yisrael, Your name**—the name of **our King—will be made beautiful with songs in every generation. For that is the obligation of all creations before You, Hashem, our God and the God of our fathers:** they must **thank You, laud You, praise You,** declare You **beautiful** and **high, worship You, bless You,** declare You **great, and sing praises** to You, **in addition to all the words of songs and praises** that were written by **Dovid, the son of Yishai, Your anointed servant.**

וּבְכֵן יִשְׁתַּבַּח שִׁמְךָ לָעַד מַלְכֵּנוּ, הָאֵל, הַמֶּלֶךְ הַגָּדוֹל וְהַקָּדוֹשׁ בַּשָּׁמַיִם וּבָאָרֶץ. כִּי לְךָ נָאֶה יְיָ אֱלֹהֵינוּ וֵאלֹהֵי אֲבוֹתֵינוּ לְעוֹלָם וָעֶד. שִׁיר וּשְׁבָחָה, הַלֵּל וְזִמְרָה, עֹז וּמֶמְשָׁלָה, נֶצַח, גְּדֻלָּה וּגְבוּרָה, תְּהִלָּה וְתִפְאֶרֶת, קְדֻשָּׁה וּמַלְכוּת. בְּרָכוֹת וְהוֹדָאוֹת לְשִׁמְךָ הַגָּדוֹל וְהַקָּדוֹשׁ, וּמֵעוֹלָם עַד עוֹלָם אַתָּה אֵל. בָּרוּךְ אַתָּה יְיָ, אֵל מֶלֶךְ גָּדוֹל וּמְהֻלָּל בַּתִּשְׁבָּחוֹת, אֵל הַהוֹדָאוֹת, אֲדוֹן הַנִּפְלָאוֹת, בּוֹרֵא כָּל הַנְּשָׁמוֹת, רִבּוֹן כָּל הַמַּעֲשִׂים, הַבּוֹחֵר בְּשִׁירֵי זִמְרָה, מֶלֶךְ יָחִיד חֵי הָעוֹלָמִים.

הַנּוֹהֲגִין לוֹמַר פְּזְמוֹנִים אֵין לְהַפְסִיק בָּהֶם בֵּין בְּרָכָה זוֹ וּבֵין בִּרְכַּת הַכּוֹס אֶלָּא מִיָּד אַחַר כָּךְ יְבָרֵךְ עַל כּוֹס ד':

Hold the cup in the same manner as during Kiddush and say the following brachah for the wine (immediately after saying the previous paragraph, without interruption).

בָּרוּךְ אַתָּה יְיָ, אֱלֹהֵינוּ מֶלֶךְ הָעוֹלָם, בּוֹרֵא פְּרִי הַגָּפֶן.

וְשׁוֹתֶה בַּהֲסִבָּה:

Drink the entire cup (or at least most of it) without interruption while seated and leaning on the left side.

וּבְכֵן Therefore, our King, may Your name be praised forever, Hashem, the strong God, the great and holy King Who is in the heaven and on earth. For to You, Hashem, our God and the God of our fathers, it is appropriate forever to offer songs and praise, praise and melody; to speak about Your might and rulership, Your power of victory, Your greatness and strength, Your beauty and glory, and Your holiness and rulership as King. It is also appropriate that we give blessings and thanks to Your great and holy name. From this world to Olam Haba, You are the only God. Blessed are You, Hashem, the mighty God and great King Who is acclaimed with praises; the God Who is worthy of thanks; the Master of wonders and miracles; the Creator of all the neshamos; the Ruler of all the creations Who chooses B'nei Yisrael's songs of praise. Hashem is the only King; He is the life of all the worlds.

בָּרוּךְ Blessed are You, Hashem, our God, King of the world, Who creates the fruit of the vine.

בְּרָכָה אַחֲרוֹנָה עַל הַגֶּפֶן:

Concluding Blessing For Wine:

(On Friday night, add the orange words.)

בָּרוּךְ אַתָּה יְיָ, אֱלֹהֵינוּ מֶלֶךְ הָעוֹלָם, עַל הַגֶּפֶן וְעַל פְּרִי הַגֶּפֶן וְעַל תְּנוּבַת הַשָּׂדֶה וְעַל אֶרֶץ חֶמְדָּה טוֹבָה וּרְחָבָה שֶׁרָצִיתָ וְהִנְחַלְתָּ לַאֲבוֹתֵינוּ לֶאֱכוֹל מִפִּרְיָהּ וְלִשְׂבּוֹעַ מִטּוּבָהּ. רַחֶם נָא יְיָ אֱלֹהֵינוּ עַל יִשְׂרָאֵל עַמֶּךְ וְעַל יְרוּשָׁלַיִם עִירֶךְ וְעַל צִיּוֹן מִשְׁכַּן כְּבוֹדֶךְ וְעַל מִזְבְּחֶךְ וְעַל הֵיכָלֶךְ, וּבְנֵה יְרוּשָׁלַיִם עִיר הַקֹּדֶשׁ בִּמְהֵרָה בְיָמֵינוּ, וְהַעֲלֵנוּ לְתוֹכָהּ וְשַׂמְּחֵנוּ בָהּ וּנְבָרֶכְךָ בִּקְדֻשָׁה וּבְטָהֳרָה. (וּרְצֵה וְהַחֲלִיצֵנוּ בְּיוֹם הַשַּׁבָּת הַזֶּה) וְזָכְרֵנוּ לְטוֹבָה בְּיוֹם חַג הַמַּצוֹת הַזֶּה. כִּי אַתָּה יְיָ טוֹב וּמֵטִיב לַכֹּל וְנוֹדֶה לְּךָ עַל הָאָרֶץ וְעַל פְּרִי הַגֶּפֶן. בָּרוּךְ אַתָּה יְיָ, עַל הָאָרֶץ וְעַל פְּרִי הַגֶּפֶן.

בִּרְכַּת בּוֹרֵא נְפָשׁוֹת רַבּוֹת עַל שְׁאָר מַשְׁקִין:

If you drank other drinks besides wine or grape juice after saying Birkas Hamazon, say the following brachah:

בָּרוּךְ אַתָּה יְיָ, אֱלֹהֵינוּ מֶלֶךְ הָעוֹלָם, בּוֹרֵא נְפָשׁוֹת רַבּוֹת וְחֶסְרוֹנָן, עַל כֹּל מַה שֶּׁבָּרָאתָ לְהַחֲיוֹת בָּהֶם נֶפֶשׁ כָּל חָי, בָּרוּךְ חֵי הָעוֹלָמִים.

בְּרוּךְ Blessed are You, Hashem, our God, King of the world for the vine and for the fruit of the vine, for the produce which grows in the field, and for the precious, good and wide open land of Eretz Yisrael that You have kindly given to our ancestors as an inheritance to eat from its fruits and to be satisfied from its goodness. Have mercy, Hashem, our God, on B'nei Yisrael, Your people, on Yerushalayim, Your city, on Tziyon, where Your glory rests, on Your Mizbei'ach and on Your Beis Hamikdash. Rebuild the holy city of Yerushalayim quickly, in our days. Bring us up to it and let us be happy in it, and we will bless You then, in holiness and purity.

May You willingly accept us as Your nation and strengthen us on this Shabbos day.

Remember us for good things on this day of the Yom Tov of Pesach because You, Hashem, are good, and You do good to everyone. We give thanks to You for the land of Eretz Yisrael and for the fruit of the vine. Blessed are You, Hashem, for the land and for the fruit of the vine.

בָּרוּךְ Blessed are You, Hashem, our God, King of the world, Creator of many living things and their needs; we bless You for all the things You have created in order to keep alive the soul of every living thing. Blessed is Hashem, the Life of the worlds.

וְאַחַר כָּךְ יֹאמַר:

Afterwards say:

לְשָׁנָה הַבָּאָה בִּירוּשָׁלָיִם

The wine in the "Kos Shel Eliyahu" is poured back into the bottle to the singing of "Keili Attah."

לְשָׁנָה May Moshiach come right away, so that **next year** we will celebrate Pesach **in Yerushalayim!**

NUSACH

We say "Leshanah Haba'ah Biyerushalayim" one time only.

MINHAGIM

It was the custom of the Rebbeim to pour the wine from the Kos Shel Eliyahu back into the wine bottle, while singing the niggun composed by the Alter Rebbe to the words אֵ-לִי אַתָּה.

NUSACH

The Alter Rebbe did not include the words "חֲסַל סִדּוּר פֶּסַח..." - the Pesach Seder has finished..." in his version of the Haggadah. This is because the emunah - belief and trust in Hashem that we develop on Pesach never ends; it continues throughout every moment of every day of the year.

Following are two incidents that happened with the preparation and printing of the תשל״ג edition:

1. The page-width of the text of the Haggadah was slightly narrower than the page-width of the explanations. When they were printed on facing pages this did not matter as it was barely noticeable. However, now that the Haggadah text and the explanations would be on the same page, it looked strange; the top part of the page was narrower than the bottom. The publishers wrote to the Rebbe and mentioned this issue. The Rebbe responded that they should make a border around the top text, which would make it the same width as the bottom text. In fact, the Rebbe selected the border design to be used.

2. At the end of the sefer, in the final sichah, the last footnote discussed the opinions of those who maintain that no brachah of "Shehecheyanu" is said at a Bris Milah. The Rebbe quotes the reason given by Tosfos, that מִשּׁוּם צַעֲרָא דְיָנוּקָא – since the child has pain, the joyous brachah of Shehecheyanu is not said.

   The sefer was given to the Rebbe before it was to be released and sold to the public on י״א ניסן, the Rebbe's birthday. The Rebbe responded on the evening before י״א ניסן that a sefer should end on a positive note. The Rebbe suggested adding the phrase, "לְשָׁנָה הַבָּאָה בִּירוּשָׁלַיִם" to the end of the sefer.

   Now, the sefarim were already printed, and it was already late at night. How could these words be added before the morning?

   A number of rubber stamps were produced with the words לְשָׁנָה הַבָּאָה בִּירוּשָׁלַיִם. That night, every sefer was stamped at its end with the words לְשָׁנָה הַבָּאָה בִּירוּשָׁלַיִם.

   The next morning, the sefarim were ready for sale as the Rebbe wanted.

After the תשל״ג edition, *The Rebbe's Haggadah* was reprinted many times. Each time, more Pesach sichos and letters were added—those that had been edited and issued by the Rebbe during that time—until finally, in 1991, the Haggadah became a handsome two-volume set.

The Rebbe's Haggadah has continued to be an inspiration, adding great depth and meaning each year to the Yom Tov of Pesach.

Appendix

About The Rebbe's Haggadah

*T*he Rebbe's Haggadah is one of the earliest sefarim of the Rebbe's teachings, and was first published in תש"ו (1946). Unlike many other sefarim of the Rebbe's teachings, which were transcribed from the Rebbe's talks (such as sichos and maamorim) and then edited and approved by the Rebbe, *"The Rebbe's Haggadah"* was actually authored by the Rebbe.

When commenting on the Haggadah, the Rebbe's astounding knowledge of all areas of the Torah came to light, because the Rebbe quoted from so many areas of the Torah, displaying a huge range of sources and references—all at a time before the invention of computer research programs!

The Haggadah was reprinted twice over the next several years, and then again in תשכ"ג (1963) in honor of it being 150 years since the histalkus of the Alter Rebbe. In this printing, the Rebbe added a number of explanations and stories connected with the Alter Rebbe. For example, the story about the Alter Rebbe searching for the chametz the entire night (page 13), and about the Alter Rebbe's Kiddush cup (page 35) were added in this printing.

In these early editions, the text of the Haggadah was printed on one side of the page, and the Rebbe's explanations were on the facing page. Being that some pages had more explanations and others less, the explanations did not necessarily face the page that contained the relevant text. Also, in those days, before computer programs, it was a tremendous amount of work to re-type and design a book. Therefore, the explanations added by the Rebbe over the years appeared as additional pages, either as an insert or at the back of the Haggadah, instead of adding them to the page where they belonged.

Ten years later, in תשל"ג (1973) the Haggadah was redesigned as a present for the Rebbe's 71st birthday. All the explanations from the previous editions were collected and reset in their correct order, and a new design was formed, in which the text of the Haggadah was on the top section of each page, and the corresponding explanations on the bottom of the page. This made the Haggadah much easier to use.

In addition, the Rebbe's public letters and edited sichos relevant to Pesach and the Haggadah were added to the back of the sefer, along with the Pesach customs from Sefer Haminhagim, making the sefer over 270 pages.

לזכרון עולם בהיכל ה׳

הנגיד החסידי הנודע לשם ולתהילה

מקושר בלו"נ לכ"ק אדמו"ר זי"ע, מחשובי ונכבדי חסידי חב"ד ושמו מפארים בכל החוגים

איש החסד והצדקה אשר פיזר נתן לאביונים, מגדולי תמכין דאורייתא

בר אוריין ומוקיר רבנן, קבע עיתים לתורה בכל עת ובכל זמן, טוב לשמים וטוב לבריות

הרה"ח הנעלה

ר׳ **ישכר דוב**

ב"ר **יונה** ע"ה

נפטר ז"ך אייר, ה'תשע"א

ולעילוי נשמת אשת חבר

האשה החשובה הצנועה והחסודה

שעמדה לימין בעלה במעשה הצדקה

מרת **מרים**

בת ר׳ **אלטער מרדכי** ע"ה

נפטרה ר"ח שבט, ה'תשע"א

וייס

ת. נ. צ. ב. ה.

לזכרון עולם בהיכל ה'

לעילוי נשמת

הרה"ח הוו"ח אי"א בעל מדות טובות
רודף צדקה וחסד

ר' שלום

ב"ר יואל דוב ע"ה
נפטר יו"ד שבט, ה'תשל"א

ורעיתו אשת חבר
האשה החשובה הצנועה והחסודה

מרת צפורה

בת ר' אברהם ע"ה
נפטרה ליל שמיני עצרת, ה'תש"ע

לפידות

ת. נ. צ. ב. ה.

נדפס על ידי חתנם ובתם

הרה"ת ר' משה אהרן צבי וזוגתו מרת העניא רבקה רות שיחיו וייס
שלוחי כ"ק אדמו"ר זי"ע, בשערמאן אוקס, קאליפורניא

לעילוי נשמת

ידידנו עוז, אחי וראשי, אלופי ומיודעי, נחמד ונעים, אהוב לכל
אשר במאור פניו קירב רבים

הרה"ת השליח

ר' יוסף יצחק הלוי ע"ה רייטשיק

בן שד"ר כ"ק רבותינו נשיאינו
ידידנו עוז
הרה"ח הרה"ת ר' **מנחם שמואל דוד הלוי** ע"ה
והרבנית מרת **לאה** ע"ה **רייטשיק**
נפטר בדמי ימיו, בשיא פריחתו בן נ"ה שנה, ביום כ"א אלול, ה'תשס"ח

ת. נ. צ. ב. ה.

נדפס ע"י

הרה"ת ר' **משה אהרן צבי**
וזוגתו מרת **העניא רבקה רות** ומשפחתם שיחיו
וייס

שערמאן אוקס, קאליפורניא

הרה"ת ר' **יונה מרדכי**
וזוגתו מרת **הדסה עלקא** ומשפחתם שיחיו
וייס

לאס אנדזשעלעס, קאליפורניא

וצדקתם עומדת לעד

זה הכותב ספרים ומשאילם לאחרים (ע"פ כתובות דף נ.)

הגדה זו נדפס ביוזמת וע"י

הרה"ת ר' **משה אהרן צבי** בן מרים

וזוגתו מרת **העניא רבקה רות** בת צפורה

שיחיו

ווייס

שלוחי כ"ק אדמו"ר זי"ע
בשערמאן אוקס, קאליפורניא

ימלא השי"ת כל משאלותיהם לטובה ולברכה, מתוך בריאות
הנכונה והשלימה, אריכות ימים ושנים טובות, והצלחה רבה ומופלגה
בכל אשר יפנו בגשמיות וברוחניות ומתוך הרחבה

ולזכות ילדיהם

שלום אליעזר, מנחם מענדל, יונה מרדכי, חנה פערל שיחיו

שיגדלו להיות חסידים יראי שמים ולומדים מקושרים
לכ"ק אדמו"ר זי"ע והולכים בדרכיו אשר הורנו נס"ו

ולעילוי נשמת הוריהם

הרה"ח ר' **ישכר דוב** ב"ר יונה וזוגתו מרת **מרים** בת ר' אלטער מרדכי ע"ה **ווייס**
הוו"ח ר' **שלום** ב"ר יואל דוב וזוגתו מרת **צפורה** בת ר' אלטער ע"ה **לפידות**

ISBN: 978-0-8266-0632-7

9 780826 606327